HAUS CURIOSITIES

The Noble Army

ABOUT THE CONTRIBUTORS

Anthony Ball is Canon Rector of Westminster Abbey and Bishop of North Africa in the Anglican Province of Alexandria.

James Hawkey is Canon Theologian of Westminster Abbey and a Chaplain to HM The King.

Tricia Hillas is Canon Steward of Westminster Abbey and Chaplain to the Speaker of the House of Commons.

David Hoyle is Dean of Westminster.

David Stanton is Canon Treasurer of Westminster Abbey.

Bashar Warda is Chaldean Archbishop of Erbil, Iraq.

HAUS CURIOSITIES

Edited and with an introduction by James Hawkey

THE NOBLE ARMY

Anthony Ball, James Hawkey, Tricia Hillas,
David Hoyle, David Stanton, Bashar Warda

Foreword by Justin Welby

First published by Haus Publishing in 2024
4 Cinnamon Row
London SW11 3TW
www.hauspublishing.com

The right of the authors to be identified as the author of this work has been
asserted in accordance with the Copyright, Designs and Patents Act 1988

A CIP catalogue record for this book is
available from the British Library

Print ISBN: 978-1-914979-01-9
Ebook ISBN: 978-1-914979-02-6

Typeset in Garamond by MacGuru Ltd

Printed in Czechia

Foreword

Justin Welby

It is a sobering thought that there have probably been as many martyrs of the Christian faith in the last hundred years as in any equivalent period in the history of the Church. The appalling slaughter visited on Christian communities in the modern age, continuing in some places even as I write, has been facilitated by modern methods of killing, even as it has ancient, barbarous continuity with the past. It is vital that Christians today continue to reflect on that history of suffering.

But the oft-quoted tag of Tertullian's about the blood of the martyrs being the seed of the Church may mislead, if it allows us to separate those who died for their faith from the mass of 'ordinary' Christians, people like you and me. The point of making much of martyrdom is surely not the death, nor even the courage of those who died, great and admirable though that may have been, but the *faith* shared with all those who place their trust in the Lord of life, the risen Jesus Christ, whose triumph over death signals God's ultimate victory of love. Every time I walk past the west front of Westminster Abbey, I'm reminded not so much of death but of the sheer power of faith that can sustain us in the darkest moments.

I am glad that Canon James Hawkey has drawn together these sermons for wider reading. Each of them takes us to the heart of one person's story of faith, one person's journey of discipleship, which shine out as examples for us all. But through those personal stories, we're also reminded of the sheer diversity of the Church today as it seeks to serve God in countries and contexts far removed from Westminster. I thank God for the vision of the Dean and Chapter of Westminster, who chose the statues twenty-six years ago so well. They have given us a lasting symbol of the breadth as well as the depth of our faith.

Contents

Introduction

James Hawkey

It has often been noted that the twentieth century saw a greater number of Christians die for their faith than any previous century, and possibly more than the previous nineteen centuries combined. The communist persecutions alone saw millions of Christian believers die at the hands of atheist totalitarianism, and other political and religious currents cut deeply and devastatingly into Christian communities across the world. The early decades of the twenty-first century have been similarly bloody; the terrifying advance of the Islamic State/Da'esh through Syria and Iraq and ethnic and religious tensions in northern Nigeria and southern Sudan are but a few examples of how the persecution of Christians has remained a contemporary phenomenon of staggering magnitude. The UK-based charity Open Doors reported that 4,998 Christians (90 per cent of them in Nigeria) were killed for their faith during 2023.[1] The Catholic charity Aid to the Church in Need reported anti-Christian violence in countries including Mozambique, Haiti, Nicaragua, and Burkina Faso in the first two months of 2024 alone.

The statues of ten modern martyrs which have surmounted the Great West Door of Westminster Abbey since 1998 are an intentionally ecumenical group, articulating the deep and rich unity to which these individuals bear witness, well beyond confessional or cultural divisions. Prompted by the persecution of Christians in the Middle East and North Africa in subsequent years, Pope Francis has frequently spoken of the 'ecumenism of blood' as a particularly powerful current in the life of the global Church. The now-famous scene on a Libyan beach in which twenty-one Christian workers kidnapped from Sirte were martyred at the hands of Islamist terrorists in early 2015 is now commemorated liturgically in both Coptic and Roman Catholic liturgical calendars. One of those executed, Matthew Ayariga, was a non-Coptic Ghanaian. His features, notably different from the others, are portrayed distinctively on icons of the martyrdom. At the time and subsequently, many sources reported that Ayariga said to his captors 'I am a Christian, and I am like them.' When he announced the inclusion of all twenty-one in the Roman Martyrology in May 2023, Pope Francis referred to their blood as 'a seed of unity for all followers of Christ',[2] developing a rich tradition which is at least as old as the Church Father Tertullian (160–240 AD), with roots in the Gospel itself (John 12:24).

The ten essays in this book began as sermons in a series preached in Westminster Abbey by the Dean and Chapter during the autumn of 2023, to mark the twenty-fifth anniversary of the installation of the ten statues of martyrs of the twentieth century. An eleventh essay is offered by the Chaldean Archbishop Bashar Warda of Erbil, Iraq, who preached in the Abbey for the Eucharist on All Saints' Day 2023, focusing on his friend and colleague Father Ragheed Ganni, martyred in June 2007. The intention behind our invitation to Archbishop Warda, who also spoke at a seminar the following day, was to highlight the contemporary reality of the marginalisation and persecution of Christians. The Noble Army is not only expansive; it is expanding.

Upon entering many of Europe's great medieval cathedrals, the visitor is left in no doubt as to whose domain they are encountering. Chartres, for example, has a massive figure of Christ in Majesty surrounded by the Evangelists and a vast company of other saints. At Cologne, the three portals of the west facade of the cathedral fan out beneath scenes from Christ's life, surrounded by statues of countless patriarchs, prophets, and saints. One of these great entrances is the Magi Portal, crowned by its carved tympanum of the Wise Men, alerting the pilgrim to the tradition that the relics of the Magi lie here. The message is clear: as you enter this ground, you enter their world, somehow encountering the kingdom of God. The scene set above the Great West Door of Westminster Abbey is more unusual, but the message is the same. Although it is an Anglican church, it is a royal peculiar and therefore is not under the jurisdiction of the Archbishop of Canterbury or the bishop of London. It is the church in which Commonwealth national days are celebrated and where visiting heads of state come to lay wreaths at the Grave of the Unknown Warrior and pray for peace. The statues of these diverse figures remind those who pass beneath them that the Church is diverse and universal, its communion stretching far beyond the boundaries of national allegiance or confessional particularity, and that in the kingdom of God those who are hated and persecuted for their faith are called blessed.

The niches beneath Nicholas Hawksmoor's great eighteenth-century towers remained empty until the early 1990s, when six of the highest spaces were filled by images of the Blessed Virgin Mary, St Peter, St Paul, St John, St Faith, and St Edward the Confessor (all saints associated with the Abbey and its chapels). The ten canopied arches immediately above the Great West Door, however, remained vacant. In early 1993, an initial proposal came from the then Surveyor of the Fabric Donald Buttress to fill these niches with statues of kings and other historical figures associated with the Abbey. The minutes of the chapter meeting in June 1993 record a discussion as to whether such statues should be 'architectural' or 'artistic' in style. But the conversation about precisely *whom* should be depicted moved on swiftly. By the end of July, the chapter had fully accepted Canon Anthony Harvey's proposal that the ten niches should contain statues of modern martyrs, not aiming to represent particular Christian confessions as such, but rather to consist entirely 'of those who have died because they were Christians or promoted Christian ideals.'[3]

By October 1993 a list of potential candidates had appeared in the chapter minutes, some ultimately depicted, others not. The subsequent discussion over the next three years displays careful interrogation of ethical, interfaith, theological, and artistic matters. Edith Stein – St Teresa Benedicta of the Cross – was initially considered to represent those killed under Nazi totalitarianism. But as a convert from Judaism, the chapter ultimately came to the view that her inclusion could be misconstrued, or offence unintentionally given to the Jewish community. Consideration was given to one of the Scholl siblings, members of the 'White Rose' student group which called for active opposition to the Nazi regime in Munich. But was their brutal execution *martyrdom* as such? Subsequently, Maximilian Kolbe was chosen to be depicted. The archive contains careful and considered correspondence around accusations levelled at Kolbe of anti-Semitism, a topic addressed in much detail by many historians since. His own record stands for itself, and Canon Harvey wrote that he considered such imputation 'unfounded' in a letter to *The Times* on 29 October 1997.

The detailed consultations and discussions of these years also record interesting questions around other personalities. It was agreed that South America needed to be represented, and Óscar Romero seemed the obvious and popular candidate. Cardinal Hume cautioned that

Romero had not been officially recognised as a martyr, making it difficult for the Catholic Church to formally approve of his depiction in this way. The correspondence eventually noted that Catholics and Anglicans handle these questions slightly differently, and the cardinal ultimately attended the unveiling.

From the beginning of the conversation it was felt essential to represent Russia, and the inspirational yet, for some, controversial figure of Father Aleksandr Men (then only recently murdered in September 1990) was discussed. Others were also suggested, including by the much-loved Metropolitan Anthony of Sourozh. Mother Maria Skobtsova, Patriarch Tikhon, and Metropolitan Veniamin (Kazansky) of Petrograd were all considered, before the chapter settled on the Grand Duchess Elizabeth Feodorovna, martyred by the Bolsheviks in 1918. Archbishop Desmond Tutu was consulted over who might best represent South Africa, and Bishop Mano Rumalshah over potential candidates from Pakistan, to avoid any allegations that the process was in some way arbitrary.

The project was ahead of its time in dealing with some subtle post-colonial dynamics. The choice of Lucian Tapiedi to represent those killed in Melanesia was considered controversial by some correspondents, who argued that the British priest Vivian Redlich, martyred by the Japanese in 1942, would be a more appropriate and recognisable figure to whom so many could relate. But Redlich was a missionary, not an indigenous Christian. Arguably, he would have been less representative of martyrs from that region. Canon Harvey addressed this directly in his letter to *The Times* in October 1997:

> Why are there no British martyrs among those to be commemorated? ... In these islands we are fortunate to have had no experience of comparable persecutions. There have of course been British missionaries and others whose Christian faith has cost them their lives abroad; but we took the view that to be truly representative those chosen should be natives of the countries in which they were martyred.

Several of these conversations played into contemporary politics. It was difficult for Dr Han Wenzao of the China Christian Council to associate himself with the project due to the inclusion of Wang Zhiming, killed during the Cultural Revolution. It was suggested in correspondence that themes of witness and service rather than persecution should be emphasised, whilst stressing that all ages and countries have examples of such individuals. Ultimately, no Chinese representative attended the unveiling, and there was a protest from the Embassy. Other questions were asked: would there be a representative of those killed during the Troubles in Northern Ireland? The Evangelical Alliance wondered whether any of those depicted could truly be called 'Evangelicals'? The correspondence filed in the archive is diverse and fascinating, and deserves further detailed scholarly attention in due course.[4]

The Dean and Chapter agreed to pay for the statues of the four virtues (Truth, Justice, Mercy, and Peace), but the commissioning of the martyrs themselves became possible through a specific gift of £100,000 from Gary Weston, via the Weston Trust. The process began with the creation of small rough models, followed by one-sixth-size models in clay and further casting in plaster, before assembling them within a full model of the niches one-third of the actual size. Plaster maquettes were then again made for carving and are now displayed in The Queen's Diamond Jubilee Galleries in Westminster Abbey. The statues were carved from two large blocks of French Richemont limestone by Tim Crawley (who designed the images), Andrew Tanser, Corin Johnson, Neil Simmons, and John Roberts, a team which had, in Buttress's words, 'a determination to revive and keep alive a gothic tradition and make a relevant twentieth-century statement.'[5]

The archive papers from this period record careful biographical, portrait, and costume research to ensure that each figure was depicted accurately and appropriately. Dominic Whitnall CR sent photos of Manche Masemola, having interviewed a girl who once shared a house with her. Dietrich Bonhoeffer's twin sister liked the idea of portraying him in a gown. There is considerable correspondence regarding Elizabeth of Russia's habit, which was designed by Mikhail Nesterov under instruction from the grand duchess herself, and the style of her pectoral cross. Tim Crawley was sent pictures of various items of Papuan clothing to ensure an accurate depiction of Tapiedi.

It had initially been hoped that the unveiling and dedication might occur during the last week of May 1997, coinciding with centenary celebrations for both St Augustine and St Columba. But by the end of 1995 it was clear that the statues would not be ready, and the service finally took place at noon on Thursday 9 July 1998, attended by HM The Queen and HRH The Duke of Edinburgh, and a panoply of church leaders, including many from the martyrs' own countries. Relatives of the martyrs were seated in places of particular honour, and included Archbishop Luwum's widow and children, Archbishop Romero's brother, two of Bonhoeffer's nieces, and cousins of both Masemola and Tapiedi. A dedicated fund had been created to help close relatives and those intimately connected with the martyrs to attend. The scriptural lessons were read by relatives of other martyrs from Iran and Papua New Guinea. Julian Filochowski, a long-standing friend of Romero, read an excerpt from a prophetic interview which the Archbishop gave just a fortnight before his murder. One of Bonhoeffer's godsons, Dietrich Bethge, played the sarabande from Bach's Cello Suite in G. Prince Philip, listed in the order of service as a great-nephew of St Elizabeth of Russia, read the account of the stoning of the protomartyr St Stephen. Ecumenically, and across the Anglican Communion, the impact was profound. Janani Luwum's successor as bishop of Northern Uganda referred to the occasion as Luwum's canonisation.

The service was surrounded by a host of other events, including a commemorative concert and a conference. The concert, punctuated by reflections from Canon Harvey, the progenitor of the project, included the world premiere of a major commissioned work by the Welsh composer John Hardy, *De Profundis*, which set lines by three of those depicted – Bonhoeffer, Romero, and Martin Luther King Jr – alongside verses from scripture. The conference included lectures from Professor Klemens von Klemperer on 'Martyrdom in a Secular Age', and from the Jesuit Michael Campbell-Johnston on Romero, entitled 'Martyrdom and Resurrection in Latin America Today.' Dr Andrew Chandler, the director of the George Bell Institute, edited a volume entitled *The Terrible Alternative: Christian Martyrdom in the Twentieth Century*, containing chapters on each of the martyrs.[6] That excellent work is largely focused on biography and offers insightful analyses of the diverse cultural contexts of each of the martyrs' sufferings. A series of Lent Lectures was given and published in 1999. This shorter book is different in character; whilst it contains elements of biography, it is primarily reflective and devotional, and the authors have intentionally avoided too many footnotes apart from when they seem essential.

A quarter of a century later, the legacy of these ten extraordinary individuals continues to speak at the heart of Westminster; their images stare down Victoria Street, silently witnessing to those who pass by. Each day, as hundreds of people leave choral evensong, many look up and enquire after their stories. When the German Pope Benedict XVI came to celebrate evening prayer during his state visit to HM Queen Elizabeth II in 2010, he was visibly moved as Dean John Hall pointed out the figure of Bonhoeffer. In January 2019 the Abbey celebrated the 125th anniversary of Kolbe's birth, at a special service attended by large numbers of the Polish diaspora. During that liturgy, three friars presented a relic of his hair to the Abbey, cut just before he was sent on his final journey to Auschwitz.

On 4 December 2018 a service was held to celebrate the contribution of Christians in the Middle East. Testimonies and reflections were given by the Greek patriarch of Jerusalem, by Sister Nazek Matty OP, forced to flee her convent in Iraq at the advance of the Islamic State, and by the Archbishop of Canterbury. HM The King, as Prince of Wales, gave an impassioned address in which he explored how those persecuted often teach the rest of the world essential lessons:

> I have met many Christians who, with such inspiring faith and courage, are battling oppression and persecution, or who have fled to escape it. Time and again, I have been deeply humbled and profoundly moved by the extraordinary capacity for forgiveness that I have seen in those who have suffered so much.[7]

At a Mass in Erbil in October 2022 Archbishop Bashar Warda told me that almost every person present would have known a martyr. During this visit, as a trustee of the charity Embrace the Middle East, I had the deep privilege of meeting many people who had fled the violent and horrendous persecution meted out to so many Christians by the Islamic State and al-Qaeda in Iraq. Many had lost families, most had lost homes. One afternoon, we visited a group of young adults in a village just north of Mosul. They spoke movingly and generously about their experiences and those of their families, about the challenge of rebuilding their lives, and how they were learning once again how to trust their neighbours. The editor's own dedication for this volume would rightly be to them.

KOLBE

Maximilian Kolbe

James Hawkey[1]

In the middle of October 2023 social media was ablaze with an offer. Amidst the horrors then emerging in the Holy Land – hostage-taking and the bombing of the innocent in Israel and Gaza – the newly created Cardinal Pierbattista Pizzaballa, the Latin patriarch of Jerusalem, had volunteered himself in a hostage swap. In particular, Patriarch Pizzaballa said in a video interview with journalists in Italy that he was willing to offer himself in exchange for children being held by Hamas. The broad public reaction was one of surprise, admiration, even amazement. Whilst this kind of selflessness is indeed worthy of our deep respect, it should perhaps be less of a surprise for a Christian leader, even an ordinary Christian disciple, to offer their life for another. 'No-one has greater love than this', teaches Jesus, 'to lay down one's life for one's friends' (John 15:13).[2]

But whilst the Christian tradition teaches us not to be surprised by such a move, our hearts beat a little more fervently when we hear or read accounts like this, partially because we begin to interrogate our own selves – 'Could or would *I* behave like that?' – but also because in this kind of situation, we sense that we are getting just that little bit closer to Christ.

St Maximilian Kolbe, the Franciscan friar canonised in 1982, was born in Łódź in central Poland in 1894. A devout child, he recalled a vision of the Virgin Mary – to whom he would have an intense devotion throughout his life – in which he had an experience which would mark the rest of his life:

> I asked the Mother of God what was to become of me, a Child of Faith. Then she came to me holding two crowns, one white, the other red. She asked me if I was willing to accept either of these crowns. The white one meant that I should persevere in purity, and the red that I should become a martyr. I said that I would accept them both.[3]

Kolbe's intellectual formation was in Rome at the Pontifical Gregorian University, but he had already entered the minor seminary in Lviv when he was thirteen. By the age of twenty he had taken his final vows as a Franciscan, and the direction of his life was clear. Upon his return to Poland, amidst regular bouts of illness, he would play a leading role in the Militia of the Immaculata, which he had founded as a prayer movement for the conversion of those considered heretics or schismatics. He was also involved in establishing the nationalist and strongly orthodox Catholic newspaper *Mały Dziennik*, an affordable daily paper published by the Franciscans of Niepokalanów, which certainly contained anti-Jewish tropes typical of the increasingly hostile atmosphere of the 1930s. Extensive research has been done to examine accusations of anti-Semitism levelled at Kolbe himself, and it is now clear that whilst he may have shared a belief in some of the appalling stereotypes unfortunately all too common in that period, there are several examples of Kolbe either refusing to publish articles by anti-Semitic authors or cautioning others to avoid doing so. One should never minimise the horrors of the legacy of what has become known as the Teaching of Contempt, and in his 2002 biography of Kolbe, Claude R. Foster argued that the 'cultural rivalry' between Jews and Catholics in pre-war Poland created a highly particular context.[4] Kolbe himself was engaged in missionary work in Japan for much of this time, returning to the major friary at Niepokalanów as guardian in 1936, from where he established a popular Christian radio station and which sheltered well over 2,000 Jews. As the power of the Nazis increased, his own publication *The Knight of the Immaculate* became increasingly critical of Nazi ideology, and September 1939 saw his first arrest. Kolbe refused to sign the *Deutsche Volksliste*, intended to create ethnically German communities across occupied territories. Signing this register may ultimately have ensured Kolbe's safety due to his German paternal ancestry, but instead he returned to the friary headquarters, which continued to shelter and hide increasing numbers of Jews fleeing deportation and persecution. The friary continued its publishing work, including much anti-Nazi material, and was finally closed in 1941. Kolbe was arrested once again by the Gestapo in February, and by the end of May he had been transported to Auschwitz.

The account of Kolbe's final days in the concentration camp is well known, amidst the infamous conditions of brutality experienced by so many Jews, Poles, Roma, gay people, Jehovah's Witnesses, Soviet prisoners of war, and other political prisoners. In late July 1941, three prisoners escaped from Kolbe's imprisonment block. In revenge and as an example to others, the deputy commandant of the camp ordered a selection of ten men to be taken to the underground starvation bunker and starved to death. One of these men, Franciszek Gajowniczek, cried out that he had a wife and children. Kolbe stepped forward, identified himself as a Catholic priest, and asked to be taken instead. Perhaps surprisingly, the offer was accepted. Later, Gajowniczek recalled,

> I could only thank him with my eyes. I was stunned and could hardly grasp what was going on. The immensity of it: I, the condemned, am to live and someone else willingly and voluntarily offers his life for me – a stranger. Is this some dream? I was put back into my place without having had time to say anything to Maximilian Kolbe. I was saved. And I owe to him the fact that I could tell you all this. The news quickly spread all round the camp. It was the

first and the last time that such an incident happened in the whole history of Auschwitz.[5]

Kolbe was one of the last of the imprisoned to die, after a fortnight of dire conditions in which he was observed by witnesses to kneel and pray without complaining while encouraging the others. His final end was delivered by two lethal injections of carbolic acid administered by Hans Bock, head of the infirmary, particularly famed for his brutality. Gajowniczek testified that he heard Kolbe say to Bock, 'You have not understood anything about life. Hate is useless. Only love creates!'[6] At his canonisation in October 1982, attended by Gajowniczek, Pope St John Paul II concluded his address on that occasion by reflecting that Kolbe's death possessed 'a particular and penetrating eloquence for our age.'[7]

How does one make sense of analysing a single death – even one of 'penetrating eloquence' – in the context of almost unfathomable killing? Even the word 'Auschwitz' has come to symbolise such depths of mass-murder and unimaginable cruelty. It perhaps feels slightly uncomfortable even to speak about the supposed serenity of a saint amid such inevitable human horror and fear. Surely, the reports testify to Kolbe's calm and focus. But one aspect which marks out *this* particular death is that it was blood given, not taken. A step forward. An arm proffered. There is a victory at the centre of this story, of a death undergone willingly out of love for another human being, reasserting the basic fact of human dignity in the face of a process designed to erase the very possibility of such solidarity. Around the time of Kolbe's beatification in 1971, some theologians argued that he should be recognised as a confessor of the faith, not as a martyr, because – strictly and formally speaking – he had not specifically been killed in *odium fidei,* in hatred of the (Christian) faith. He was, however, a martyr of charity; 'through laying down his life', Pope John Paul II said, 'he made himself like Christ.'[8]

One particularly powerful mystery at the heart of the Christian Gospel, which we see with a certain kind of clarity in the lives of the martyrs, is that we will save our lives by losing them. We hear this from the lips of Jesus in all four Gospels; the synoptics each have a version of the saying, whilst St John uses the image of a grain of wheat falling into the ground and dying before it bears much fruit. Another prisoner who survived Auschwitz, Jerzy Bielecki, later testified that Kolbe's death was 'a shock filled with hope, bringing new life and strength ... It was like a powerful shaft of light in the darkness of the camp.'[9] In God's economy of grace and gift, in which nothing is lost and in which we know, to use a phrase attributed to Hans Urs von Balthasar, that God himself is 'personified handing-over', there is a new kind of life, a new creation unveiled in such a sacrifice. Of all the central Christian images, finding your life by losing it is one of the least comfortable or comforting for those of us privileged to live relatively undisturbed lives. But we should recall that etymologically, the call to martyrdom is simply a call to witness, and we can only witness within our own contexts. Kolbe himself only published one article for *The Knight*, just prior to his final arrest in 1941. It was a call to witness, at once both profound and provocative. 'No one in the world can change Truth', he wrote,

> What we can do and should do is to seek truth and to serve it when we have found it. The real conflict is an inner conflict. Beyond armies of occupation and the hecatombs of extermination camps, there are two irreconcilable enemies in the depth of every soul: good and evil, sin and love. And what use are the victories on the battlefield if we ourselves are defeated in our innermost personal selves?[10]

Kolbe's ultimate context, at the end, was a place of brutality and nihilism, where extinction was the programme and the intention. He was attuned to the moment of choice, the moment of witness, and being so, found that this pinnacle of his life gave life. At the canonisation, Pope John Paul II spoke of this moment as a distilled message of hope for all such contexts of hatred and violence: 'A victory was won over all systematic contempt and hatred for mankind, and for what is divine in mankind – a victory like that won by our Lord Jesus Christ on the cross.'[11]

In one starvation block, buried in the mud and mire of abominable human hatred, this life *given* teaches us nothing less than the Christian Gospel in one moment, in all its fullness.

MASEMOLA

Manche Masemola

David Hoyle[1]

I was invited to Ely Cathedral to preach for their saint: that staunch Saxon princess Etheldreda. Ely is a cathedral that makes a landscape. It commands the view, changes the scenery, and shifts your mood. The cathedral was built on what was once an island in a shifting bed of reeds. Once it was a lost place; you could hide there. Now it is visible for miles around, rising out of the fens as though it might go on rising forever. Ely is a grand, raw-boned building that tells believers that they are dwarfed by glory. It is wonderful, but it is also a place of personal association. This is the cathedral in which I was ordained. Ely is a place of memory and history to me; it ties me to my past and roots me into faith and conviction.

Place matters. The place you call home, the views you grew up with, remind you of what you believe and why. No surprise then that in scripture place matters a lot. The Old Testament keeps telling us that God is met in places where the memory of the meeting lingers on – a burning bush, Mount Sinai, Beth-El:

How awesome is this place! This is none other than the house of God, and this is the gate of heaven (Genesis 28:17).

The ministry of Christ is a mission that issues out preaching and teaching; it is a lot of words. Properly understood, it is more than that – it is memory and it is an itinerary of place names and references to vineyards, fields, hillsides, and the sea. Faith is Bethlehem, Jerusalem, Golgotha; it is Rome, Assisi, Canterbury, and Westminster. The places matter, they are a necessary part of the story we tell. The poets have always understood this: R. S. Thomas urges us to turn aside and pay attention, Edwin Muir sees far and near the fields of paradise, and T. S. Eliot brings us to our knees where prayer has been valid. Make no mistake, Christian faith is not an idea, nor is it an aspiration. Christian faith is character, and character always has a time and a place.

Character, time, and place are the only ways we can tell the story of Manche Masemola. So, we must identify the correct place and the right time. She is the youngest of the modern martyrs set above the Abbey's Great West Door. Her place, in that excellent company, is second from the left. A good place to be, but her home was once in what is now South Africa. She came from Northern Transvaal, north-east of Pretoria. And it is there that she died in 1928.

Masemola belonged to an ethnic group called the Pedi. They were an ancient people who used to control great swathes of land under the leadership of a paramount chief. The heavily armed ambition of Boer trekkers and the British Army changed all that. A long, familiar, and depressing story of colonial settlement drove the Pedi back into hill country, which was less fertile and prone to drought. Worse, the Pedi, who had an inclination to live in peace with their neighbours, tried to reach an accommodation with the early settlers. They made agreements with them and made space. The Pedi had no sense that a person could 'own' land that they believed was clearly there to be shared. They were baffled, then dismayed, and then angry to discover that these brash settlers had arrived thinking that they had all become little kings and queens.

So, Pedi sovereignty was lost, the land was lost, and dignity was lost. The British began to tax the people whose livelihoods and sovereignty they had stolen. Money could now only be made by leaving their homelands and going to work for white bosses in the mining industry. That was, therefore, where many young men went. Some of them left for good, turning urban and strange to their parents in the process. In this sad story a people became estranged from their home and from one another. Communities that never had to consider what home and ownership might mean became troubled by questions of who did and did not belong, and who was foreign. The white missionaries, arriving with the Gospel, stepped straight into difficulty. These missionaries brought medicine and new skills, but they were also foreigners with a bright confidence of their own about the Church and the number of the faithful. It seemed that their aim was to destroy the communities they came to serve. Individuals might turn to Christ, but villages were troubled by the divisions that the new faith introduced. Pedi converts quickly found that their neighbours now called them 'heathens' or identified them as alien and 'foreigners'. To become Christian was to accept another identity that made you a stranger within your own country and family.

It was in this place, and this time, that Masemola converted to the Christian faith. Details of her life are scant. We are not even sure of her date of birth; it is usually suggested that she was born in 1913.[2] Aged about thirteen, a cousin took her to the settlement at Marishane to hear a missionary preach. She was impressed and asked her mother for permission to go more regularly. So began a long and increasingly bitter struggle within the family. Masemola's parents had traditional and local beliefs – to begin with, they fended off Christian influence by making their daughter commit to the traditional initiation school for young women. From the beginning, Masemola experienced Christian allegiance as a contest between cultures. To adopt a new faith was to set yourself apart. To others it looked like defiance and disloyalty. It was disruptive of relationships and all the ties that bind. Masemola was also engaged to a young man, one of the migrant workers who had been forced to live far from home, and she was told to wait for him to return to the village. She refused and her disobedience was a source of outrage, which started a cycle of violence. She was argued with, beaten, and forced to drink a traditional remedy intended to heal her. Still she went to hear the preacher.

This young woman was made of stern stuff. She was not deterred by ill treatment; in fact, it seemed to strengthen her commitment. Very few of her words survive but the preacher at Marishane reported that she spoke of being baptised in her own blood, 'a better baptism' as she called it. She knew that her faith would lead to her death. We know that she said, 'If they cut off my head, I will never leave my faith.'[3] Permission to travel to Marishane was soon refused, but Masemola continued to pray morning and night. Finally, on or around 4 February 1928, her parents took her beyond the limits of their village and beat her brutally. The young girl dragged herself away into the bush. She died alone, propped up against a stone. In a bizarre continuation, her parents, finding her body, attempted to bury her in the village cemetery, but digging in what was usually soft earth, they hit rock. They tried again and again, but turned up rock. She was not going to be theirs, even in death. So, Masemola was carried back to the distant hill where she died and interred by the stone where they found her.

The old hostilities battled on. Christian faith was contested, community was ruptured. In the mission at Marishane, a memory of faith and courage persisted and pilgrims began to make their way to Masemola's grave.

Her mother remained defiant for long years after that brutal death, urgently warning people of the danger Christians posed. Then, remarkably, she was herself converted and baptised, making a first communion in 1969. Was that a reconciliation of a sort? I cannot tell you; a heavy silence falls on Masemola, her family, and the problem of divided loyalty.

So, what words do we find now about our modern martyr? Tracking down Manche Masemola, I looked at the Church of South Africa website and found a flyer for the annual pilgrimage to her grave. The picture offered there was our own statue on the west front of the Abbey.[4] Our commemoration in Westminster now shapes the story of this resolute young woman. She was a stranger in her family and village and is indeed a stranger to us. Yet, her story and ours grow together.

There are, I think, two things to keep in mind. First, we must be honest about her 'otherness.' Her place and time are so different from ours, and her bright, brittle courage and the test it faced are unfamiliar. The saints are also the 'other'. To manage their strangeness, we too often tame them with casual descriptions, putting them into catalogues or lists in which they keep even stranger company. Those lists intend to tell us that there are types of sanctity. There are even types of *royal* sanctity into which we can slot our own Saint Edward:

Some were crowned again by martyrdom ... others chose exile from their homeland ... yet others reigned

with justice and holiness ... Among [them] ... King
Edward shone like the morning star in a cloudy sky.[5]

The Epistle to the Hebrews knows this trick, naming the
distinct and the different with a surer touch:

> They were stoned to death, they were sawn in two,
> they were killed by the sword; they went about
> in skins of sheep and goats, destitute, persecuted,
> tormented – of whom the world was not worthy
> (Hebrews 11:37–38).

In that place and that time Manche Masemola is witness
to a faith that can be brave and startling; a candle in the
dark, a witness against prejudice and violence. Yet, secondly, she is also a girl, a daughter, and a friend to some.
Strange to us in one way, she is still one of us, her story
and ours finding points of contact.

That is what the saints do for us. They show us a faith
that can be ours and utterly human, and they show us too
how courage, faith, and holiness can, and must, make us
strange – men and women who find a home not here,
but in the city that is yet to come (Hebrews 13:14).

LUWUM

Janani Luwum

Anthony Ball[1]

For those of a certain generation, the name Idi Amin conjures up images of the worst type of power-hungry and brutal despotism. His 1972 expulsion of around 80,000 South Asians with ninety days' notice grabbed headlines and had a significant impact on migration to the UK – the fiftieth anniversary of this event was marked by a reception in Buckingham Palace in November 2022.[2] Amin was the third president of Uganda, taking power in a military coup in 1971 and eventually being deposed by invading Tanzanian forces in 1979 after he attempted to annex part of that country. In Amin's Uganda, human rights abuses were rampant, alongside nepotism, corruption, and gross economic mismanagement. The political repression, ethnic persecution, and extrajudicial killings carried out under his rule resulted in an estimated 80,000 to 500,000 people being killed, one of whom was Archbishop Janani Luwum.[3] As with all those depicted above Westminster Abbey's Great West Door, he speaks to us as powerfully today as he did then and at the time of his martyrdom.

The scripture readings in this reflection give us some pointers to the significance and story of Archbishop

Luwum. Zechariah's experience after protesting against those in power who were not following God's commandments, that 'they conspired against him, and by command of the king they stoned him to death' (2 Chronicles 24:21), has obvious parallels with Luwum's death at Amin's hands. St John the Divine writes in Revelation, 'I, John, your brother who share with you in Jesus the persecution and the kingdom and the patient endurance' (Revelation 1:9); this could even be a quote from the former Archbishop of York, John Sentamu, who has said that 'the day [Luwum] died I resolved to be ordained.'[4] And as the Abbey Choir sing in Psalm 119:158, 'It grieveth me when I see the transgressors: because they keep not thy law', we might hear Luwum speaking not only of his challenges to President Amin but also of his own conversion to Christianity.

Luwum's conversion took place in January 1948 amidst a phenomenon known as the East African Revival, of which the public confession of personal sin was a sometimes-controversial feature. It happened in his home village of Mucwini, in the northern Ugandan Kitgum District near the Sudanese border, while listening to a sermon by Yusto Otunno. Luwum was about twenty-five years old and a schoolteacher, like his father Elijah – himself an early convert to Christianity. Feeling himself convicted and having twice broken out in a heavy sweat, when it happened a third time 'he confessed Jesus Christ as his Lord and in tears repented of his sins, crying aloud'[5] and then said 'Today I have become a leader in Christ's army. I am prepared to die in the army of Jesus. As Jesus shed his blood for the people, if it is God's will, I will do the same.'[6]

Luwum began preaching, especially against excessive drinking and smoking, which was ruining many lives and seemed to be ignored by church catechists. 'It grieveth me when I see the transgressors: because they keep not thy law.' His uncomfortable and uncompromising message addressing sin, salvation, and the need for repentance – in the personal as well as the societal sphere – soon landed him in trouble with both civil and Church authorities, resulting in a period in prison.

Within a year, with Yusto's encouragement, Luwum acknowledged that God was calling him to sacrifice his teaching career and the real possibility of being a local chief, so that he might give himself to full-time ministry in the Anglican Church. He left behind his wife, Mary, and their young daughter to go and study in Buwalasi Theological College, becoming first a lay reader, then a deacon, and, in 1956, a priest. He came to study in the UK in 1958, returning a year later as vice-principal of Buwalasi and then, after a further two years' study in England in the early 1960s, as principal of the College. In 1966 Luwum was appointed provincial secretary of the Church of Uganda, Rwanda, Burundi, and Boga-Zaire. Although his role was complicated by tribal tensions, he distinguished himself as an early advocate of the first ten-year plan supporting a vision of a self-governing, self-sustaining, and expanding Church. A vision, incidentally, offered by the first Anglican bishop to take up residence in 1890, Alfred Tucker.

In January 1969 Luwum was consecrated as the bishop of Northern Uganda in Gulu, the town to which as a boy he had walked eighty miles to attend high school. The Ugandan President Obote and the (Muslim) chief of staff of the army, one Idi Amin, were both present at the service. As a bishop, Luwum's ministry focused not only on preaching and spreading the word of God, but also on the holistic development of people and communities, founding schools, health centres, hospitals, and a dairy farm. His warm and generous personality was profoundly visible in his care for refugees from both Rwanda and Sudan. He saw himself as serving all people, a shepherd after the model of Jesus, the Good Shepherd.

Lord Sentamu notes that in 1973, when he was posted as a judge to Gulu, it was an area that had 'suffered greatly from political and military oppression [and] ... had more widows and orphans at that time than elsewhere in Uganda.'[7] As well as asking him to be chancellor of the diocese, Luwum told Sentamu, 'We must be Christ to these people: be their advocate and take up their cases. The local prison is filled to capacity with innocent people'.[8] Sentamu did this, and after his own imprisonment later fled to the UK, making his own the scripture, 'I, John, your brother who share with you in Jesus the persecution and the kingdom and the patient endurance' (Revelation 1:9).

Already outspoken against the growing excesses of Amin's regime, including involvement in the drafting of a World Council of Churches protest after the expulsion of

Ugandan South Asians, Luwum was elected archbishop in 1974. Even though the Church of Uganda, Rwanda, Burundi, and Boga-Zaire also suffered from the tribal rivalries and internal divisions apparent in society, Luwum continued to exercise a ministry for all, often calling on Ugandans to live together peaceably and in harmony while personally interceding with Idi Amin against some of his excesses and abuses of authority. 'It grieveth me when I see the transgressors: because they keep not thy law.'

In standing up to the president's authority Archbishop Luwum could be seen as drawing on the witness of the Ugandan martyrs of the 1880s. Their martyrdom took place in the context of a three-way struggle for power within the Buganda Royal Court between animists, Christians, and Muslims. King, or Kabaka, Mwanga II had already ordered the killing of the incoming Anglican bishop, James Hannington. He then asserted his authority over the young and educated Christians in his court, including by exercising traditional royal demands of sexual submission. Men lying together being against their religious convictions, these demands were rebuffed and, combined with the political factors and personal grudges at play, this insubordination led to the execution of twenty-two Roman Catholic and twenty-three Anglican converts: 'they conspired against him, and by command of the king they stoned him to death'.

President Amin was not one to accept challenges to his authority or style of governance. Early in 1977 there had been a small rebellion within the army, and although quickly overcome, the reprisals were extensive. In February 1977 Archbishop Luwum's house was subjected to an early-morning raid, ostensibly to search for hidden weapons. There were none. He delivered a letter of protest, signed by most of the Ugandan Anglican bishops. Amin responded by producing his own letter, supposedly confirming Luwum's participation in a plot against him. Luwum and two cabinet ministers, also committed Christians, were arrested and, with six other bishops, faced a military trial on 16 February and were summarily condemned. As Luwum was separated from his colleagues and led away, he said to them, as Jesus did so often in his earthly ministry, and echoing the voice of the 'one like the Son of Man' in Revelation 1:4–18, 'Do not be afraid.'

They did not see him again alive. The car carrying Luwum and the two cabinet ministers allegedly suffered an accident. Although his body was absent from his memorial in the capital (which was attended by around 4,500 mourners), once returned, the sealed coffin was opened and the body was discovered to be covered in bullet holes. Again, 'they conspired against him, and by command of the king they stoned him to death.'

An international outcry followed the news of Archbishop Luwum's murder, marking what was probably the zenith of Idi Amin's regime. Within two years Amin was ousted, evading justice and ultimately seeking refuge in Saudi Arabia. He died in 2003.

In a 2016 sermon honouring Luwum, Archbishop

Justin Welby noted that martyrdom is the ultimate witness to the truth of Christ.[9] The Church of England follows the Anglican Communion's liturgical calendar in commemorating his death on 17 February. Luwum's life and death inspire us to recognise the ultimate sovereignty of Christ, the first and the last, the Alpha and the Omega, and to examine our own lives in this light. We all face choices: to speak or to be silent, to collude or to confront, often in contexts that may not seem to have anything religious about them. But our moral response should be informed (or not) by our Christian conscience, by our willingness to acknowledge or deny Christ.

In the Parable of the Sheep and the Goats (Matthew 25:31–46), when the goats are sent away from the king it is not because they were not religiously faithful at a critical moment, but because they failed to act justly in feeding the poor and clothing the naked. In both his actions and his speech, Luwum was an uncompromising witness for what he saw as God's justice and love. Our own times are rife with complex issues that do not immediately present themselves as specifically religious ones – refugees, ceasefires, international aid, the environment, social inclusion. In each, our individual response needs to be informed by our Christian faith. What will cause us to say, 'so far and no further'?

May Janani Luwum inspire us not to conform to the powers of darkness but rather to seek to transform the world for 'the Lord God, who is and who was and who is to come' (Revelation 1:8).

ELIZABETH

Elizabeth of Russia

James Hawkey[1]

On 2 April 1908, a memorial cross was dedicated in Moscow to Grand Duke Sergei, governor of the city and uncle of Tsar Nicholas II, who had been assassinated at that spot three years earlier. Grand Duke Sergei's life, personality, and legacy have been much disputed, but those of his widow, the Grand Duchess Elizabeth, have been widely celebrated and deeply admired. At Elizabeth's commission, the inscription on this huge memorial cross, seven metres high, was simply the Gospel text, 'Father, forgive them, for they know not what they do' (Luke 23:34).

Princess Elizabeth of Hesse had arrived in Moscow for her marriage in 1884 at the age of twenty. A granddaughter of Queen Victoria, raised as a Lutheran but with an Anglican mother, she was related to many of the royal and noble houses of Europe. She is a great-great-aunt of King Charles III. It was Elizabeth's own choice to convert to Orthodoxy just before Easter 1891, a decision which would become a watermark for the rest of her life and a faith which would become more intense in extraordinary ways after her husband's assassination.

Hers was a life that can be seen in two halves: the first as a court beauty, a princess of great style and wealth, and one of the most eligible women in Europe; the second as a religious superior and a resolute witness to the depths of God's love in Christ.

The night before her husband's funeral, Elizabeth asked Moscow's prefect of police to escort her to Taganka Prison to meet the assassin, Ivan Kalyayev, a member of the Socialist Revolutionary Combat Organisation, which had previously assassinated two ministers of the interior. Her sister, Princess Victoria of Hesse, recalls in her unpublished memoirs that Elizabeth had hoped this would be a secret encounter in which she might awaken the assassin to repentance.[2] However, the then French ambassador to the Imperial Court, Maurice Paléologue, recounts a version of the meeting and the tone of their subsequent correspondence in his memoirs. Elizabeth spoke to the prisoner not as a princess but as a widow, and gave Kalyayev a copy of the Gospel, with a request that he read it. Some accounts state that Elizabeth then offered to intercede for him with the tsar if he would repent. Although Kalyayev refused, Elizabeth wrote anyway seeking a pardon. Different narratives of Kalyayev's attitude towards a plea spread throughout Moscow, and Paléologue records that Elizabeth received a letter from the prisoner which reads as follows:

I did not say I am sorry, because I am not. If I agreed to hear what you had to say, it was only because

I regarded you as the unfortunate widow of a man
whom I had executed ... The account you have given
of our interview is an insult to me. I don't want the
mercy you have asked for me.[3]

This tragic story with its all human and political complexity sets before us the Christian imperative to forgive,
whilst also focusing the human heart on the need to
learn how to *accept* forgiveness. It was Archbishop
Desmond Tutu, writing from the much later context
of a different kind of violent political and ethical landscape, who famously said that there could be no future
without forgiveness. As South Africa emerged from the
horrors of apartheid, Tutu reflected that forgiveness had
to trump not only retributive justice but even restora-
tive justice.[4] Only forgiveness can open a space in which
seemingly irreconcilable contexts and histories can turn
a page. Only reconciliation can do the work. The only
final medicine for hatred is love.

This kind of love bore extraordinary fruit in Elizabeth's
life and orbit. The trauma of assassination and widow-
hood were channelled with huge energy and determination into a project of imagination and Christian
generosity. She sold all her jewels and in February 1909
opened the Convent of Saints Martha and Mary (or, the
Marfo-Mariinsky Convent) in Moscow, a religious house
where women could take temporary vows whilst serving
the sick and poor. When the convent was opened and
the first sisters received, she said to them 'I am leaving

the brilliant world where I occupied a high position, and now, together with all of you, I am about to ascend into a much greater world, the world of the poor and afflicted.'[5]

Hers was a new model in the Russian Orthodox tradition, and members of the community would often leave the convent with a wide range of skills. After the example of Martha and Mary, the two sisters of Bethany and friends of Jesus, Elizabeth's vision was one both active and contemplative. The convent was a church and medical centre rolled into one – a devout life of Orthodox prayer underpinned a shelter, a pharmacy, an orphanage, and a hospital. It was said that Elizabeth took her religious vows even more seriously than her marriage vows, and her decision to enter the religious life was one which created tension amongst the imperial family and high society. The only member of her family to be present on the occasion of her religious profession was her sister, Princess Victoria. Their mother had consulted Florence Nightingale about the foundation of a women's health association called the Alice Women's Association for Nursing (*Alicefrauenverein für Krankenpflege*) in Hesse, which although a secular institution followed the model of a religious motherhouse, and in some ways the grand duchess's vision for the Marfo-Mariinsky Convent was surely influenced by the interweaving of these themes.[6] Furthermore, familiar with the activities of Western deaconesses, the rule of the convent spoke of its sisters following the ancient example of the 'holy myrhh-bearers and deaconesses.' Elizabeth added her voice to those already proposing the restoration of the rank of deaconess in the Russian Church as a distinctive participation in its pastoral life. During the Marfo-Mariinsky Convent's peak years, between 1914 and 1917, around 150 sisters were members of its community, working in healthcare and amongst the homeless poor of Moscow. Despite its closure by the Bolsheviks in 1926 after years of pressure, and the exile of eighteen of the remaining sisters to Turkestan in central Asia, the sisterhood was re-established in 1994, two years after Elizabeth's glorification as one of the New Martyrs of Russia.

It is clear from all the sources that Elizabeth had the character of a charismatic religious founder, and that she used her influence and energy to create a unique kind of community. Her own personality was right at the heart of this. Her sister Princess Victoria recalled how patients would often ask for Ella – as Elizabeth was known – to be present with them during their last hours. Victoria wrote in her memoirs,

> In one case the husband, who was very devoted to his wife, was a communist, and he and Ella each held the hand of the dying woman. The husband afterwards said to one of the nurses 'that if all the members of the Imperial Family were like this one, the first one he had ever met, his opinion of them would be different.'[7]

But this status amongst many of the poorest of Moscow was not sufficient to save her. After the tsar's abdication in 1917, she was relieved of all her charitable responsibilities apart from the convent. An offer of sanctuary came from the kaiser via the Swedish ambassador, which she refused. On 7 May 1918, the third day of Easter, Elizabeth was arrested and accompanied by one of her sisters, Varvara, to Alapayevsk. On the day after the murder of the tsar, Elizabeth and Varvara were thrown into a mineshaft, into which grenades were then dropped. The precise circumstances of their martyrdom are still contested, and they may have been killed beforehand. One soldier present testified that as Elizabeth was seized, she cried, 'Father, forgive them, for they know not what they do.' When her body was exhumed two years later, an icon of Christ, given to her on the day of her religious profession, was found on her chest alongside two unexploded grenades. In a final journey of astonishing length and complexity, she was ultimately buried on the Mount of Olives in Jerusalem, yards from where Jesus himself prayed and was betrayed on the night before he died. The sisters' confessor, Father Mitrofan, who was entrusted with oversight of the convent after Elizabeth's arrest in 1918 until the community's dissolution at the order of the government in 1926, was sent to the camps of the gulag for sixteen years and finally exiled. He too has been proclaimed one of the countless New Martyrs of Russia.

The first monument in the Moscow Kremlin to be destroyed after the October Revolution of 1918 was Grand Duke Sergei's memorial cross with that inscription, 'Father, forgive'. Forgiveness is fragile: to forgive is always a choice, an active decision which, if embraced, can liberate and lead to a new future. Elizabeth's life, including her death, shows us that from forgiveness can emerge new possibilities, bearing rich fruit which would otherwise be impossible. We might call such a world the New Creation, because its origin is found within the reconciling love of Christ himself, which pours out from the cross. Learning how to forgive, and how to accept forgiveness, especially in contexts of complexity and confusion, is often the work of a lifetime. But it is a work which gives life, and which robs the grave of its victory.

KING

Martin Luther King Jr

David Stanton[1]

Martin Luther King Jr is one of the most well-known religious figures depicted above Westminster Abbey's Great West Door and is particularly celebrated for teaching his followers techniques of nonviolent resistance, examples that are still used today. Through a combination of faith, deep intuition, and Gandhi's philosophy of nonviolence, he fought for justice through peaceful protest. In doing so he delivered some of the twentieth century's most iconic speeches, and he is the only American, other than George Washington, whose birthday is a national holiday. His famous 'I Have a Dream' speech in 1963 was a defining moment for the American Civil Rights Movement, which in turn gave birth to the Civil Rights Act of 1968. In this speech he shared a dream that people should not be judged by the colour of their skin, but rather by the substance of their character.

In 1954, King became pastor of the Dexter Avenue Baptist Church in Montgomery, Alabama. Two years later, after the Supreme Court had declared laws of segregation unconstitutional, he was arrested, subjected to much personal abuse, and even experienced the degradation of having his own home bombed. Three years later he was elected president of the Southern Christian Leadership Conference, and at the age of thirty-five he became the youngest recipient of the Nobel Peace Prize.

On the evening of 4 April 1968, he was assassinated on the balcony of a motel room in Memphis, Tennessee. A year before his assassination he had travelled to Newcastle University in the UK to receive an honorary doctorate in civil law. At the ceremony he said to a spell-bound audience,

> As you well know, racism is a reality in many sections of our world today. Racism is still the coloured man's burden and the white man's shame. And the world will never rise to its full moral or political or even social maturity until racism is totally eradicated. Racism is exactly what it says. It is a myth of the inferior race; it is the notion that a particular race is worthless and degraded innately and the tragedy of racism is that it is based not on an empirical generalisation but on an ontological affirmation. It is the idea that the very being of a people is inferior.[2]

Like the other chapters in this book, this reflection began life as a sermon. On the day it was preached, Sunday 10 December 2023, we marked the seventy-fifth anniversary of the Universal Declaration of Human Rights. This enshrines the fundamental belief held by King that all human beings are equal in the sight of God, regardless of race, colour, religion, sex, language, political opinion, birth, or other status. The UN theme for 2023 was 'Freedom, Equality and Justice for All', and we recognise that his bravery lives on today. Despite all progress made, the struggle for genuine equality remains both incomplete and urgent.

Today, fifty-five years after his assassination, racially motivated hate crimes are still the highest reported type of hate crime in the UK. Indeed, the death of George Floyd back in May 2020 sparked global outrage and continues to call for greater urgency in confronting systemic inequalities. King continues to remind and challenge us that hope and humanity must overcome aggression and inhumanity.

As he said,

> We know through painful experience that freedom is never voluntarily given by the oppressor; it must be demanded by the oppressed.[3]

His challenge to inequality was underpinned by a deep and living Christian faith, and this faith in Godly justice was expressed in his belief that all people are created in the image of God. The contemporary Church of England still needs to take this seriously. The 2021 Archbishops' Anti-Racism Taskforce report 'From Lament to Action' calls for urgent changes to the broad culture of the Church and emphasises a flowing 'not from identity politics but from our identity in Christ.'[4] It speaks of how the sin of racism disfigures God's image in each one of us, how it dehumanises people by taking away their fundamental God-given human dignity.

King expressed this when he said,

> Wherever racial sin flourishes systematically, either in society or in our church, we must challenge it together. We must repent of racial sin, turn away from racism and be reconciled, so that we may all experience the love of God.[5]

He taught that such sin is ultimately characterised by a failure to recognise the image of God in the face of every individual, whatever their background, and a failure to treat everyone with the dignity that God's image deserves. He drew our attention to the fact that the Gospel calls us all to continually confront the idolatry of racism and the evils in our world and 'to proclaim justice and mercy as we seek to walk with our God' (Micah 6:8).

Recognising that Christ himself lived on Earth during violent times, King identified this as offering a radically positive approach to social injustice. He regularly reminded his listeners of the primary Christian commands to be grounded in Christ and to constantly recall how Christ unfailingly preached God's unconditional love, a love which welcomes and forgives. His fundamental philosophy of nonviolence – identified in his first book, *Stride Toward Freedom*, and replicated within so many of his sermons and speeches – was grounded in how Christ taught his disciples to love their enemies (Matthew 5:44) and to turn the other cheek (Matthew 5:39); how he intervened to stop the woman caught in adultery from being stoned by her accusers (John 8:1–11) and how, on the night before he died, he told Peter to put away his sword (Matthew 26:52).

Through combining his inspiration from Christ with techniques learned from Gandhi, King embraced them together within a code of life. This special and very personal code of life had six principles: first, nonviolence is courageous because it's strong in spirit, mind, and emotion; second, nonviolence embraces reconciliation and understanding; third, nonviolence recognises that those who do wrong are also victims; fourth, nonviolence that involves suffering (without retaliation) really does educate and transform society; fifth, nonviolence chooses love rather than hate; sixth, nonviolence has deep faith in a God of justice and love.

Although nonviolence initially appeared to many to be weak and inefficient, in the face of oppression this position is now wholeheartedly supported by huge numbers of people today, who recognise that 'injustice anywhere is a threat to justice everywhere.'[6] But as we are painfully aware, this has not always been the case – certainly not during the 1960s, when King became a very divisive figure.

During that decade, 75 per cent of Americans disapproved of him speaking out against the Vietnam War and economic disparity, and many white Americans believed he was doing more harm than good in promoting the fight for civil rights. Since then, nonviolent resistance has been a key strategic tool in the hands of the marginalised. Nelson Mandela used it to great effect against apartheid and the Black Lives Matter movement has used it with considerable success across society, especially within the fields of policing, government, and education.

As we mark the seventy-sixth year of the Universal Declaration of Human Rights, we do so with Martin Luther King Jr in mind. We give thanks for his life, courage, and teaching. We recognise with gratitude that his dream lives on and his message of social equality remains prescient.

ROMERO

Óscar Romero

Tricia Hillas[1]

On 24 March 1980, the Archbishop of San Salvador, Óscar Romero, was officiating at an early evening mass in the chapel of the Divine Providence Hospital. Poignantly, the Gospel reading came from the twelfth chapter of John:

> The hour has come for the Son of Man to be glorified. Very truly, I tell you, unless a grain of wheat falls into the earth and dies, it remains just a single grain; but if it dies, it bears much fruit. Those who love their life lose it, and those who hate their life in this world will keep it for eternal life. Whoever serves me must follow me, and where I am, there will my servant be also (John 12:23–26).

Romero gave the homily, and Philip Berryman describes what followed as a car drew up outside:

> As Archbishop Romero began the offertory ... a marksman took aim through the doorway, and fired one shot. It hit the archbishop in the heart. He fell

at the altar and was rushed to an emergency room where he died. The Salvadorian legal system made no significant investigation into the murder. Three days after the murder, two men attempted to kill the judge to whom the case would be assigned and he fled the country.[2]

Rumours have persisted about who ordered, and who carried out, the shocking shooting. Suspicion has surrounded wealthy business owners, politicians, and military death squad commanders who felt threatened by the Archbishop's outspoken criticism of the country's military dictatorship. Yet, more than four decades after his murder, the killers remain free.

Berryman suggests that,

... in asking who killed Oscar Romero, the specific individuals are of less importance than the kind of political, geopolitical and ideological climate that for years could have justified the sacrifice of dozens, then hundreds, then thousands of people.[3]

How did we get to this point? Seàn-Patrick Lovett writes,

Oscar Romero's father wanted his son to become a carpenter. With good reason. As a child, young Oscar had a talent for fixing things that were broken.[4]

Lovett observes that when Romero became Archbishop of San Salvador in 1977, El Salvador was broken; so many lived in poverty, while an elite group held all political and economic power to their own advantage, and death squads ensured things stayed that way.

Romero was seen as a safe choice by the elites, unlikely to cause much trouble. But trouble was all around. Just three weeks after he was appointed Archbishop Romero, his good friend, Jesuit Father Rutilio Grande, was murdered by one of those death squads. Five more priests would be assassinated over the next three years.

After the military seizure of power in 1979, Romero began broadcasting weekly radio sermons. And this is the first key point I would like to highlight: when it was needed, and at great personal risk, Romero spoke up and he spoke out.

He spoke first and foremost out of his faithful attending to God's word, and then he spoke to the oppressed, to their oppressors, and into the brokenness of his country. He spoke and would not keep quiet, and since he understood that there could be no justice without truth, Romero determined to speak the truth. At a time when few official communications were trusted he provided a weekly summary, gathering reports of disappearances, murders, and attacks and giving voice to eyewitness testimonies. His homilies opened up the message of Jesus: one of love, radical forgiveness, and the need for open justice.

In 1980 El Salvador descended into a civil war, which

would last for twelve years and leave over 75,000 people dead. As the conflict began, Archbishop Romero set up pastoral programs to assist victims of oppression and became even more outspoken in condemning human rights violations.

As shepherd to all the people of El Salvador, Romero spoke directly to each and every one, out of his deep conviction that each person was the beloved of God. He said,

> There is no anonymous person among us who are here. All of you have your own individual histories, even the humblest of persons, even the smallest child, even the poorest and sickest folks listening by radio, all those people about whom nobody will talk in the history books. God has loved each of you singularly, as an unrepeatable phenomenon.[5]

Romero spoke to the elites, the military, the government; to landowners, plantation owners, businessmen; to National Guardsmen and agricultural workers; to seasonal coffee pickers and mothers; to all the people. He taught the poor that they could hope, work, and pray for God's coming kingdom of love and justice, now and throughout their lives, and sought to guide them to choose the peaceful path to the kingdom and not the way of violence. He called upon those in power to be mindful of the justice, compassion, and truth to which God called them.

Romero made a special plea towards the military, imploring them to stop killing their own people. 'No soldier is obliged to obey an order that goes against the law of God', he said, 'I beseech you. I beg you. I command you! In the name of God: "Cease the repression!"'[6] He voiced these particular words in what would be his last radio broadcast, given the day before he was killed.

Romero's relentless preaching of both justice and peace earned him the description of the 'voice of the voiceless'. But not everyone found what he said to be palatable. At one point his radio station studio was bombed.

Some accused the Archbishop of meddling in what they believed did not concern him, of meddling in politics. Doing so, and therefore seeking to drive a wedge between the kingdom of God and the kingdoms of the world, between faith and politics, they missed the point. Jesus had called his followers to love their neighbour and to hunger and to thirst for the kingdom of God. Richard Harries has reflected that the love of neighbour has an inescapable political dimension and that it is naive to think that we can love our neighbour without being concerned about the decisions and public policies which affect so much of their lives and opportunities, for good or ill.[7]

This is the second key point to note: that Archbishop Romero, being compelled to speak, stepped into a space which brought faith and the public sphere face to face. He engaged there, where divine concern and justice met pressing human need and pain.

'I want to affirm that my sermons are not political', Romero said. 'Naturally they touch on politics and they touch on the reality of the people, but their aim is to shed light and to tell you what it is that God wants.'[8]

Romero longed for those in power to see their people as brothers and sisters, each made in the image of God. He described the painful reality of their lives as 'so dense.'[9]

Romero urged Christians to bring the redemption and transformation of Christ into the midst of the world. In so doing, he stood in a long line of Christian social reformers, including anti-slavery campaigners, housing rights advocates, prison reformers, American civil rights activists, and anti-apartheid campaigners. Romero defended the freedom for all to be active in El Salvadorian politics. Today, here in the UK, many people who serve in our own Parliament and in local politics across the country draw deeply on their faith as they seek to serve their neighbour.

But Romero also understood that political enterprise and new policies alone could not provide sufficient solutions to El Salvador's problems. All true change begins with the heart and what was needed was a conversion of hearts. Shockingly, this was needed even amongst some who were associated with religious faith. Romero was well aware that amongst the influential leaders who gave the orders for the cruel disappearances and brutal killings were those from Catholic and Evangelical families and communities.

Romero's own hope and earnest desire was to see a community of truth and love fashioned by God, even out of those who had once been enemies. All this was rooted in his own character, built up through his faith over many years. Roberto Morozzo Della Rocca writes,

> He was a bishop with a lofty sense of responsibility, who was deeply moved at the sight of bloodshed ... Romero was not a rationalist, nor was he a politician. Rather he was a man of intense feelings, a man of prayer who experienced history as a journey towards God.[10]

And this is the third key point I hope to convey: that the Gospel of Jesus Christ was the meaning, the strengthening sinew, and the aim of all that Romero did for the people and the God whom he served. Della Rocca again argues,

> It was because of the faith that Romero spoke about reconciliation, loved the poor and demanded social justice ... It was because of the faith that he invited all to conversion and pointed out the sin of his contemporaries. It was because of his confidence in the gospel that Romero did not take cover from the threats, did not abandon his faithful, did not retreat, but accepted the death that he then knew was certain.[11]

Over and over again Romero pointed to Jesus, telling how he had come to Earth in poverty and had endured the pain and humiliation of the cross before the triumph of the resurrection. Setting the self-giving of Christ upon the cross before all present and those listening on the radio, in that last homily, moments before he was shot, Romero said,

> May this body that was immolated and this flesh that was sacrificed for humankind also nourish us so that we can give our bodies and our blood to suffering and to pain, as Christ did, not for our own sake but to bring justice and peace to our people.[12]

As the gunman's bullet found its target, evil forces sought to silence their turbulent priest. How little they understood.

Jose Osvaldo Lopez, an Anglican in El Salvador, put it this way:

> With the life and works of Romero, I am certain that Jesus himself passed through El Salvador ... Romero is for me not simply a pastoral model but above all an enormous challenge, one that requires me as a Christian to assume a critical attitude against social and structural injustice. Yet Romero does not only challenge me to denounce injustice. Above all; he invites me, calling on me forcefully, to love those around me.[13]

BONHOEFFER

Dietrich Bonhoeffer

Tricia Hillas[1]

On 27 July 1945, people gathered in London for a service which may have seemed improbable to some. Two months earlier, the war in Europe had ended; Hitler was no more, and the Allies declared victory. News of Nazi atrocities was filtering through.

At the outset of the war, it had seemed possible in public discourse to distinguish between the German people and the National Socialist Party. However, as Allied casualties mounted, nuance faded and public focus settled on one, apparently uniform, hated enemy.

In July 1945, with the conflict in Europe only recently over, it seemed remarkable that a memorial service should be held in London, and moreover broadcast on the BBC, for a German, killed three months earlier. That German was the theologian and Lutheran pastor Dietrich Bonhoeffer.

Theologians and historians have spent lifetimes evaluating and elucidating Bonhoeffer's legacy. One reflection is not the place to cover such impossibly expansive ground. Instead, we shall turn to aspects of Bonhoeffer's letters, written while he was a prisoner of the Nazi regime.

Arrested in 1943, Bonhoeffer spent the next two years in Berlin prisons, before heavy Allied bombing led to a transfer to the Flossenburg prison camp, where finally he was hanged. In these confusing closing days of war, word of their fate emerged only very slowly.

So it was, Eric Metaxas explains, that on that 27 July 1945 an elderly couple sat in Berlin with their radio tuned to the BBC.[2] The husband was the most prominent psychiatrist in Germany; both had opposed Hitler from the beginning and were proud of their family's resistance. Though war in the European theatre had ended, news of loved ones was scarce. At length the couple heard about the death of their son, Klaus, but of their youngest son, Dietrich, there was no news. Rumour reached them that he'd been seen – alive. Then a neighbour told them that the BBC was to broadcast a memorial service the next day – it would be for Dietrich. This was how they learned of his death.

They had learned of his life and reflections through his letters from prison. Many of these letters had been written by Bonhoeffer to his parents, whilst others were sent to his close and dear friend Eberhard Bethge. It is to themes within these letters that we now turn. These include the human experience of time, the undertow of despondency, agency, and powerlessness, both human and divine, and the elements which sustain hope.

Writing to his parents on 15 May 1943, Bonhoeffer explained,

One of my predecessors here had scribbled over the cell door 'In 100 years, it will be over'.[3]

This needful trust, that even the worst will one day pass, reflects both the cobweb-like fragility of our lives and the steadfast comfort of ever-flowing time.

Time, especially the 'feeling of time', occupied Bonhoeffer's thoughts as he waited for developments in his case, with so many false dawns and setbacks. In his letters he muses on the tension between the consolation known by the psalmist, who could say of God, 'My time is in your hands' (Psalm 31:15) and yet also give voice to the heart-wrenching cry, 'How long, O Lord, how long?' (Psalm 13:1).

Bonhoeffer's letters in themselves mark out the passing of time. With references to nature's changing seasons, he speaks of the warmth of summer and the chill of winter. But it was the familiar cycle of the Christian year – Holy Week, Easter, Ascension, Whitsun, Advent, Christmas – which gave shape to his life and writings in prison. His thoughts explored their theological and liturgical meanings but also stirred rich memories of family associated with these times. The liturgical seasons also gave a richness to Bonhoeffer's stark present. He wrote of Advent, for example, with its waiting, hope, and occupying of self with 'this, that or the other' being a fitting image of life in his prison cell.[4]

In those cells and in his letters, as Bonhoeffer wrestled with the switching back and forth of hopeful signs and setbacks, he grappled with further profound tensions such as that between calm composure and shocked despair, and between agency and powerlessness. In terms of agency, finding himself imprisoned Bonhoeffer also discovered that his dependency on others was clear. His letters contain very ordinary requests, for books mostly – they express deep gratitude for gifts, including cigarettes and flowers from the garden, and concern about the needs of the gift-givers.

In a letter to his parents of 13 September 1943, he notes,

> It is a strange feeling to be so completely dependent on other people; but at least it teaches one to be grateful, and I hope I shall never forget that. In ordinary life we hardly realise that we receive a great deal more than we give, and that it is only with gratitude that life becomes rich. It is very easy to overestimate the importance of our achievements in comparison with what we owe to others.[5]

At times Bonhoeffer writes of progress in his studies and of the riches of scripture, whilst at other moments he notes his inability to concentrate and how he has left the Bible untouched. This is no smoothed-over hagiographical account, but rather a man coming to terms with the immovable walls and limits of life. Yet, as noted by Sam Wells, out of this came a deeper openness to vulnerability and powerlessness, even that of God.[6] We see something of this in a letter Bonhoeffer wrote to his dear friend Eberhard on 22 December 1943. As he was writing, their earnest hope that he would be released for Christmas was fast evaporating. Bonhoeffer writes,

> I can (I hope) bear all things in faith, even my con-
> demnation, and even the other consequences I fear,
> but to be anxiously looking ahead wears one down.
> Don't worry about me if something worse happens.
> I must be able to know for certain that I am in God's
> hands, not in men's.[7]

This entrusting of his fate into God's hands, not his own, not even those of his captors, is a mark of Bonhoeffer's freedom, even within his imprisonment, and of his life, even when death came.

So, imprisoned, not freed, he crafted prayers for his prison companions to use – a gift to them that Christmas – and in his letters he wrote of nature, beauty, music, art, theology, and philosophy. His appreciation of these and his intellectual voracity opened his prison cell to the outside world and far beyond.

In ways which remind me of Tolkien's Shire and its homely hobbits, Bonhoeffer's letters from prison bring together the understated glory of the homely and ordinary (woollen jumpers and birdsong) with hopes for a transcendent future and a time when evil would be vanquished.

Bonhoeffer had urgent plans for a future he was certain would come, but which he knew he might not live to see.

These dreams, like those of others imprisoned for faith – John the Baptist in Herod's cells, Jesus himself, Paul and Barnabas, John exiled on Patmos, John Bunyan, and Dr Martin Luther King Jr – would prove to be impossible for tyrants and oppressive regimes to extinguish.

'Please don't ever get anxious or worried about me, but don't forget to pray for me – I am sure you don't!'[8] Bonhoeffer wrote in a later letter, adding,

> I am so sure of God's guiding hand that I hope I shall be always kept in that certainty. You must never doubt that I'm travelling with gratitude and cheerfulness along the road where I am being led.[9]

That road would lead through, not simply to, his execution on 9 April 1945.

A month later Germany surrendered. The war in Europe was over. The earlier prisoner, who had written on the wall of Bonhoeffer's cell, was right – in far fewer than 100 years the Nazi regime was over. And yet, as we remember Bonhoeffer and the other martyrs honoured in this series, we remember those imprisoned and persecuted for their faith today. In 2019 the then foreign secretary, Jeremy Hunt, commissioned the Right Reverend Philip Mounstephen, then bishop of Truro, to review the Foreign and Commonwealth Office's support for persecuted Christians. The report describes in harrowing detail the scale of the suffering and the imperative for all of us not to look away.[10]

Bonhoeffer, writing from prison, asked his family and friends never to forget to pray for him, confident that they would indeed never forget. May his witness and their faithfulness spur our own constancy, that we may be equally steadfast in our prayer and aid for our sisters and brothers in this, our own time.

ESTHER JOHN

Esther John

Anthony Ball[1]

Twenty-six years ago, when the late Queen Elizabeth and her husband, the Duke of Edinburgh, unveiled the ten statues of twentieth-century martyrs above the Great West Door of Westminster Abbey, the then sub-dean, Anthony Harvey, told those assembled:

> There has never been a time in Christian history when someone, somewhere, has not died rather than compromise with the powers of oppression, tyranny and unbelief. But our century, which has been the most violent in recorded history, has created a roll of Christian martyrs far exceeding that of any previous period.[2]

The sad fact is that it seems most likely that our own century will exceed that grim record. I want to share with you the story of one of those ten martyrs from the last century – Esther John – and reflect a little on her contemporary experience in her homeland.

She was born Qamar Zia in 1929 and grew up in a Muslim home in Madras (modern-day Chennai), India, as one of seven children. She attended a government school until she was seventeen, when her father's illness prompted a transfer to a nearby Christian school. In 1947, shortly before Qamar's eighteenth birthday, the state of Pakistan was formed, created as a homeland for Muslims of the subcontinent, and the family moved to Karachi – the capital of the new state. Although she was at that school in Madras for only a short time, it had a huge impact on her life. She later said of the experience,

> Just as soon as I set foot in this school I noticed a Christian teacher who was different from anyone I had ever known. I saw her gentle way of speaking, her kindness to all the students and her great faithfulness in her work. Her life made so deep an impression on me that I was really puzzled. 'How could any human being be like that?' I wondered over and over again. Later I realised that it was all because God's Spirit was in her.[3]

The life of that unnamed teacher is a lesson to us all in our own context. It brings to mind the exhortation often attributed to St Francis of Assisi, to 'preach the Gospel at all times, and if necessary use words.' It was that life and a lived-out witness to Christian values that planted a seed in Esther's mind and heart that was to germinate, grow, and bear great fruit.

We all come to know about Jesus Christ because someone told us about him; that person in turn only knew about Jesus because someone had told them, and so on, in a succession going right back to the Apostles, who, in turn, had been told by Jesus to 'Go, therefore, and make disciples of all nations, baptising them in the name of the Father, and of the Son, and of the holy Spirit, teaching them to observe all that I have commanded you' (Matthew 28:19–20). This statement by Jesus is known as the 'Great Commission' and it places as important an emphasis on the mission for the church today as it did for that school in Madras.

Although there was daily Bible study at the school, Esther said, 'At first I did not study with zeal, but rather indifferently. I had heard the Christians called blasphemers, and I did not like even to touch their book.' However, one day, while trying to memorise part of the Old Testament, Isaiah 53, she added, 'God, by his grace, showed me that there was life and power in this book. Then I began to realise that Jesus is alive for ever. Thus God put faith in my heart and I believed in Jesus as my Saviour and the forgiver of my sins. Only he could save me from everlasting death ... whereas before I thought that my good life could save me.'[4]

Notice here how she says that it was God who put faith in her heart rather than any human agency. As an important Anglican Communion document puts it,

[The] desire to see others come to Christ is a primary motivation of mission, and when the Holy Spirit works within the heart of our neighbours to bring them to faith in Jesus, we will rejoice. We always remember, though, that this is the Spirit's work, not ours, and we repudiate any attempt to coerce or manipulate people into conversion.[5]

Centuries of religious violence and wars, as well as the witness of scripture (including that recorded in 1 Maccabees 2:15–29), all point to the futility and consequences of compulsion or coercion in matters of religion. The gentleness, humility, and joy with which Esther went about sharing her Christian faith provides a telling contrast to such violence but, as we shall see, did not protect her from it.

But I'm getting ahead of where we are in the story. Qamar, as she still was at this stage, did not tell her family about her newfound faith and they soon left for Karachi. She wrote to one of the teachers in her school in Madras to tell her of the move, and that teacher contacted Marian Laugesen, a missionary in Karachi. Amazingly, Laugesen managed to find Qamar amidst the thousands of refugee settlers and visited her. When her mother and aunt were out of the room Qamar explained that she had had to leave her Bible in Madras and asked Laugesen to bring her a New Testament. This she did about a fortnight later, passing it over hidden amongst her school textbooks, shortly before being transferred away from Karachi.

For the next seven years Qamar had no contact with Christians but continued to read her New Testament secretly. It was only when her parents set about arranging a marriage for her that she ran away from home. It was June 1955. In a culture where a wife submitted absolutely to her husband and normally lived with her parents-in-law, to whom both she and her husband would have submitted, she knew that it would be quite impossible for her to live as a Christian if married to a Muslim.

Marian Laugesen had returned to Karachi and was working in an orphanage, where Qamar was given refuge and began to work, taking the name Esther John. Her family were very angry and, for her safety and to avoid the accelerated plans for her marriage, she moved north to Sahiwal in the Punjab. There she lived in the nurses' home of a Christian hospital, working there and being baptised in its chapel. She was soon sent to train at the United Bible Training Centre in Gujranwala, where she stayed until 1959. She visited her family twice in that time and she was warmly received, with little pressure put on her.

After finishing her Bible training Esther went to live in Chichawatni, a small town near Sahiwal. She stayed with an elderly American couple, the Whites. She and Janet White travelled together to the surrounding villages, on foot or bicycle, doing Evangelistic work. They would spend five or six days in each village teaching the Bible to the small community of Christians, who were very poor, mostly illiterate, and shared their pastor with perhaps a dozen other villages.[6] Although Esther was high-born, she was delighted to share the lives of

Christians of low-caste origin (which was not always the case in the subcontinent, then or, indeed, in our own day). She put considerable effort into teaching a number of illiterate Christian women to read, hoping thereby to break the vicious circle of poverty and ignorance.

By this time Esther had received several increasingly insistent letters asking her to return home. Having already refused four arranged marriages (itself an extraordinary and brave achievement), around Christmastime she wrote back by registered post setting out two conditions under which she would return – first that she would be allowed to live as a Christian, and second that she should not be forced into marriage against her will. There was no reply.

On the morning of 2 February 1960 Esther was found dead in her bed in the Whites' home, her skull smashed twice. She was buried in the Christian cemetery in Sahiwal. The police suspected a disappointed lover but an exhaustive search for evidence produced only the observation to Dale White, 'Sir, we have found no clue. This girl was in love only with your Christ.'[7] Despite two police enquiries her murderer was never identified.

In contemporary Pakistan the situation for Christians and other religious minorities remains precarious, despite the protections of religious freedom guaranteed by the country's constitution. A sad consequence is that non-Muslim women and girls are constantly at risk of sexual assault, abduction, and forced conversion. This was brought to the attention of the world in 2020, when thirteen-year-old Arzoo was taken from her parents by a forty-four-year-old Muslim man. Two days later, her father was informed that the abductor had produced a marriage certificate stating Arzoo was eighteen and had converted to Islam. A court gave custody to the 'husband.'

A particularly problematic, indeed infamous, area is the application of blasphemy laws that were brought in during the 1980s under the rule of General Zia-ul-Haq. Pakistan's penal code mandates the death penalty or life in prison for anyone defiling the name of the Prophet Muhammad and life imprisonment for desecrating the Quran. These laws are increasingly being leveraged to accuse Christians and other non-Muslims of insulting the Prophet Mohammed or the Quran. The case of Aasiya Noreen, better known as Asia Bibi, rose to some prominence a few years ago. In 2009 she had been accused of blasphemy after an argument with some co-workers while harvesting berries, and about eighteen months later she was sentenced to death by hanging. Her case attracted worldwide attention and, eventually, in 2019 she was released and fled to Canada, before claiming asylum in France. Before that, in January 2011, the governor of the Punjab, Salman Taseer, was assassinated by a bodyguard for his support of Bibi and opposition to the blasphemy laws. The minister for minority affairs, Shahbaz Bhatti, a Christian, suffered the same fate two months later. A memorial service was held for him in St Margaret's Church, Westminster Abbey, a fortnight after his assassination.

False accusations are often made to target people after an unrelated dispute, and even a false accusation can lead to mob violence. In August 2023, for example, in Jaranwala in the Punjab province, two Christians were accused of blasphemy and a local eyewitness said that 'In the blink of an eye, the mob went from 100 people at one location to 4,000 people at various Christian [communities] all over Jaranwala and nearby locations.'[8] At least twenty churches were burned or looted, along with many Christian homes.

Such pressures and persecutions faced by our Christian sisters and brothers in many parts of the world put into perspective our own trials in witnessing to the Christian faith and values in an increasingly secular and sometimes hostile environment. It is not for nothing that Jesus said, after giving the Great Commission, 'I am with you always, until the end of the age' (Matthew 28:20). Indeed, out of the eleven Apostles charged with that Commission, by tradition only St John died of natural causes. The rest were martyrs. Experiences like Esther's are not unique, in Pakistan or elsewhere in the world, even if they are not widely known. Yet, as the theologian Tertullian observed in North Africa in around 200 AD, 'The oftener we are mown down by you, the more in number we grow; the blood of Christians is seed.'[9]

TAPIEDI

Lucian Tapiedi

David Stanton[1]

As a young child I can distinctly recall stories of brutality, pain, and murder. Before Japan entered the Second World War my mother and her parents lived in Penang, but when the Japanese invasion took place in 1941 they, like many other expatriates, fled the country. They had to escape very quickly, hurriedly burying valuable items in the garden. On his return, my grandfather encountered first-hand people who had suffered greatly at the hands of the occupying forces. Friends had been murdered and others had been victim to unspeakable atrocities. The Japanese conquest of South-East Asia was a brutal war, at times even turning indigenous populations against themselves.

Very similar things happened a few months after the invasion of Penang, when the Imperial Japanese Army invaded Papua New Guinea in January 1942 with 350,000 troops. In comparison to Penang, the Papua New Guinea occupation was far more brutal and many more lives were lost. Later, US Marine Robert Leckie, in his memoir *Helmet for My Pillow*, described encountering an entire village of native people, men, women, and children, who had fled the Japanese:

Some were hobbling on rude crutches made from sugar cane, some – the ancients – were borne aloft on litters, some were supported by the more stalwart among them; all had been reduced by starvation to mere human sticks.[2]

Unlike many others, Lucian Tapiedi consciously made the extremely brave and heroic choice to stay and care for his fellow countrymen rather than travel to safety. It was this act of personal self-denial in the face of imminent danger that ultimately led to his death. Tapiedi was an extraordinary Christian man, who was highly obedient to his bishop and did the work that he fervently believed God had called him to do. In January 1942, in response to the invasion, Philip Strong, the Anglican bishop of New Guinea, instructed Anglican missionaries to remain at their posts. Here is part of what he said in a radio broadcast on 31 January 1942 at 3.30 p.m.:

My brothers and sisters, fellow workers in Christ, whatever others may do, we cannot leave. We shall not leave. We shall stay by our trust. We shall stand by our vocation. We do not know what it may mean to us. Many already think us fools and mad. What does that matter? If we are fools, 'we are fools for Christ's sake.'[3]

He was not to know that the New Guinea campaign would be one of the hardest-fought of World War II.

American and Australian forces relied heavily on native Papuans to achieve victory.

Lucian Tapiedi was born in either 1921 or 1922 in Taupota, a village on the north coast of Papua New Guinea. He was a teacher at mission schools before entering St Aiden's teacher training college at Dogura in 1939. In 1941 he joined the staff at Sangara, near Kokoda, as a teacher and Evangelist and had only been there for a few months when the Japanese invaded.

He could have escaped, but on the advice of his bishop he chose to stay in order to protect his people and the missionaries with whom he worked. When their village was attacked and they were under severe threat, he led his people deep into the jungle, from where, at high personal risk, he would venture back alone to civilisation to collect food and supplies. At some point, however, the group decided to find safer ground and moved from their place of hiding towards the coast.

The circumstances of Tapiedi's death are unclear. I doubt we will ever know the full details, but one oral account records that he had been asked to return to the mission to retrieve some money and supplies and was killed on this expedition. Nevertheless, two facts are clear and well known: firstly, he was axed to death near a stream by Kurumbo village, and secondly his killer was not a Japanese soldier, as many first thought, but a local Papuan man called Hivijapa. As in so many theatres of war, the boundaries between indigenous population and invading force often become blurred and complex, with need and starvation often leading to compromise. Collaboration is as old as war and the occupation of foreign territory.

Hivijapa most probably sensed an inevitable Japanese victory. With Tapiedi dead, the remainder of the faithful were rounded up by the locals and handed over to the Japanese, and after brutal interrogation six were beheaded, including a young boy. Some were buried, some were thrown into the sea. Tapiedi was buried at Sangara. We may well recall that betrayal and religion have met before: the kiss of Judas; David's betrayal by a close friend; or perhaps when Ahithophel and his son Absalom turned against him.

This is a dreadful and heartbreaking story, but one with an ending full of faith. The man who brutally murdered Tapiedi was never brought to trial, returning instead to his community and carrying on with his life. Sometime later, after brutally axing Tapiedi to death, Hivijapa was converted to Christianity and was baptised, taking the baptismal name of Lucian. He had become a local architect and designed and paid for the building of a church at Embi dedicated to the memory of Tapiedi. By all accounts he embraced the Christian faith and became an active member of the church council. The church of St Lucian formed an important part of his personal penitence and repentance. The church flourished and soon become a diocesan centre until its destruction following a volcanic eruption in 1951. It was then then rebuilt at Popondetta and continues to serve the Church, not least through offering ministerial training.

The concept of martyrdom is as old as Christianity itself, but the martyrdom of Lucian Tapiedi and the conversion of Hivijapa are complementary aspects of our common pilgrimage of faith. Here we see again how Christ himself served as the prototype of finding strength through weakness and achieving victory through defeat. We would do well to remember three things: first, that many of the early faithful, including all but one of the Apostles, were martyred; second, that the Church not only venerates its holy martyrs, but is regenerated by their sacrifice; and third, that the martyrs' intercession, reigning in heaven with Christ their King, is now even more powerful than their bearing witness here on Earth. Their prayers strengthen and fortify us so that we in turn may have the courage to lay down our lives for God. Their contribution to the future of the Church is beyond measure, because it is the gift of one's entire life, 'even [to] death on a cross' (Philippians 2:8).

Today, the vast majority of Papuans identify with some denomination of Christianity. The moving account of the witness and short life of Lucian Tapiedi has undoubtedly led many others to faith in Christ. May his example and fellowship continue to do so.

WANG ZHIMING

Wang Zhiming

David Hoyle[1]

If we are going to know anything about Wang Zhiming most of us are going to have to put in some hard yards. We need to go to a place seldom visited and to a time and experience that are both profoundly unfamiliar. Frankly, he was not like us, his life beyond the common experience of most worshippers in Westminster Abbey. We need to begin in Yunnan in the mountains of south-west China, near the border with Myanmar. This is where one of China's ethnic-minority communities live, the Miao people. It is a long way off; rough country, contested in every sense. In a long persecution the Miao people had been driven into the badlands and near despair. Nineteenth-century Protestant missionaries used to say that 'hopelessness was the way of life.' Perhaps that is why the Christian Gospel spread quickly there. In 1907 over 1,400 Miao people were baptised. Twenty years later there were 20,000 Christians and by the 1950s there were well over 100,000.[2]

So, we are in an awkward space where identity is up for grabs and ideas shift. A new faith changed life and culture. The Miao developed a written language simply in order to translate scripture. They also developed a musical voice for their faith. So, Christianity became local, but teaching still spoke in the accents of foreign missionaries. But this is not a history lesson; we need to note the encounter between different cultures and move on. Changing political fortunes in China created new loyalties and made new enemies. Foreign missionaries were expelled by the now-Communist state in 1949, but Christian churches were not banned. In Yunnan, the Communists suddenly insisted that the Chinese were one nation and that the old tribal persecution was over. That was true up to a point. New prejudices shouldered out old hatred as landlords were denounced and the Party pressed for further revolution.

It was in this endless contest, in this push and pull – never over, never the same – that Wang grew up. He was a teacher and an Evangelist in a local church. When the foreign missionaries left, he became a leading figure and was ordained.

He believed in the God revealed in Jesus Christ, and he also believed in a Chinese Church, a local Church. We know that in the early 1950s he supported Communist Party policy. As such, he signed up to the 'Three-Self Patriotic Movement', promising that the Church would never be an agent of the old imperialism; his loyalty to nation and party was tested and he conformed. He went to Beijing and he met Chairman Mao. That, however, was an accommodation that could only go so far. In 1958 the government line hardened into an 'Anti-Rightist' campaign. There were fresh persecutions and in Yunnan the Church was driven underground. Wang was now labelled an anti-revolutionary, and in May 1969 he was arrested and imprisoned. His crime was simply that he would not join the endless spirit of division, he would not condemn. He was minded to forgive, he sought reconciliation. He believed in life, not death. The party, however, wanted to know that he would take sides. In China they called his love of the life that we share 'anti-Party and anti-socialist activities under the cloak of religion.'[3]

This is quite recent history, yet we know surprisingly little, and what we do know is debated. There is clearly more than one version of events. It seems Wang had an enemy: a local, lapsed Christian who had joined the Red Guards, a man with a personal grudge – quick to denounce, quick to accuse. Where believers saw constancy, he saw obduracy. The big stories, the stories of faith and martyrdom, are like this; they are of grand narrative, but they are also personal and worked out in a place, a time, and a web of relationships. In such a place and time as that, Wang was sentenced to death. The day before the sentence was carried out his family were permitted to see him. Freedom of expression was impossible and Wang needed to choose his words carefully. He admitted that he had not been able to reform his thinking and then said, 'you should follow the words from above.'[4] It was a simple testimony, but a decisive glimpse of his commitment to a truth that surpasses all other loyalties – words from above.

On 29 December 1973, Wang was dragged before a mass rally of more than 10,000 people and executed. It was meant to frighten and subdue the Christian population. Instead, the crowd rushed the stand where officials were seated and denounced them. Then, for long years, religion, both Christian and Muslim, was suppressed. Only when Chairman Mao died was a greater tolerance possible. The Sapushan church that Wang had cared for was rebuilt and then, not far from his home, an inscribed tablet was erected, reading:

> Learning from the shining example of Jesus Christ, glorifying God and bringing benefit to people was his life's work. He loved his country and was dedicated to the church although he endured many storms.[5]

That tablet is the only known monument to a Christian victim of the Cultural Revolution. Wang's story is still not well known. It is part of the marvel of those statues on the west front of the Abbey that they confront us with the bigger picture of martyrdom, they show us more than we first knew. The very different stories that make up this book ask us to think about what martyrs are and what martyrdom means. And the obvious truth is that martyrdom is varied – worked out differently in each place, in each time, and in a particular web of relationships.

That lonely memorial to Wang Zhiming in Yunnan tells you that there is no cult of martyrs in China. There, they do not want to dwell on the defiance or bravery of a witness facing persecution. They do not tell those stories of defiant personal witness. To do that would too easily make Wang the outsider who refused to conform to the state. He could so easily become an Evangelist for something foreign, a spokesperson for the faith from England, a Christian who was not Chinese. That was never Wang's belief.

We began this reflection knowing that we needed to go somewhere unfamiliar and wrestle with things not known. That is fundamentally part of what we have to understand if we are to understand martyrdom. You see, the temptation is to tell these stories as though we are describing giants of the faith, mythical creatures braver, bolder, better than us. That is not why the martyrs matter. They are not strangers. The martyrs are just like you and me, they are people who follow Jesus of Nazareth, living lives worked out in different times, beds of relationships, and in ordinary places across the world – a hospital chapel in Central America perhaps, a motel in Memphis, or on the outskirts of a village in Papua New Guinea. They live the slow, steady consequences of a life of faith until it ends unexpectedly in a mundane act of violence. These are people like us, our kin; they remind us that the world and our human lives are shot through with God's grace and that all too often we do not see the glory and the gold.

Yes, of course, our martyrs were men and women of courage, so shaped by truth that they could not deny it.

They were all, like Wang, unable to reform their thinking. They matter because that same truth breaks out over and again, in different places, and against the odds, as the eternal, ceaseless love of God – always and everywhere the same. That truth, that love, overcomes our myriad differences and draws us all into the saving life of Christ. Martyrdom is not grand theatre, nor myth; it is the slow consequence of accommodations and acts of commitment slowly mounting up until identity is forged, then named and known. It is the consequence of a faith that supplants the identity we find in a particular community with the character that comes from a life in Christ. Meeting the martyrs, we are confronted with differences of time and place, with things unfamiliar and not known, and yet we also encounter familiar truths that bridge all that divides us.

As we reflect on the witness of this particular martyr, from a place few or none of us know, from a time of unfamiliar battles, and in a language we do not understand, we hear a voice speak as it spoke to Wang Zhiming. And we find we recognise it after all, and that it speaks to us too.

God Will Wipe Away Every Tear

Bashar Warda[1]

The liturgy we celebrated together on All Saints' Day 2023 honoured the lives of the martyrs who walked paths of holiness to bear witness to the love of Christ. The readings on that occasion centred on the theme of praising God and thanking him for his love for us, from the depths of our hearts, minds, and with all of our strength and gifts. He loved us so much that he sacrificed his only Son for our sake. In response to this love we try to respond with all our hearts, souls, minds, and might by being close to him; to get to know him. If our bodies prevent this unity, we must offer them to him, just as he offered his body for us, to make us holy, believing that life is lived with Christ and in Christ.

The martyrs stand eternally as witnesses in their supreme love for God; a love founded in Christ's love for us, the one who gave his life like a grain of wheat so that we may live life to the full. They made the moment of death an opportunity to sacrifice themselves for him and to strengthen the faith of their brothers and sisters. Their eyes were fixed on one face, the face of Christ, their souls free from every barrier which might threaten this unity.

Our Lord Jesus did not call us only to listen to his word but invited us to have a deep and constant relationship with him, to unite with him. It is not about knowing *of* Christ, but to know him personally; then many graces will be given to further that relationship. Therefore, martyrdom is not only a sacrifice we make, but rather is borne of the fruit of he who first loved us and planted the great seed of his love within us. This testimony is essential for building the Church, the Body of Christ.

St Paul the Apostle wrote, 'This is a faithful saying: if a man desires the position of a bishop, he desires a *good work*' (1 Timothy 3:1). The reason was that the bishop was often the first to receive martyrdom, and one who desired to be a bishop needed to be prepared for martyrdom and unity with Jesus Christ. Therefore, our Eastern Chaldean Church ensured that the relics of the saints and martyrs were preserved in a special place; special hymns are chanted for them every day during morning and evening prayers. When the Church celebrates the ordination of a bishop, this celebration is considered a major feast for the Church. The prayers begin on Saturday evening and the elected bishop is asked to sit in the House of Martyrs (where the relics are enshrined), praying there, reflecting on his service, in which he must be prepared to unite with Jesus, to be a martyr. To this day, in the Assyrian marriage rite, when a young man and woman come forward to marry before the altar, a tiny portion of dust from the House of the Martyrs is mixed in a cup of wine and presented to the bride and bridegroom. They also are called to show a martyr's witness in their marriage covenant, striving together to emulate Christ and the Church, as taught by Paul the Apostle in his letter to the Ephesians about the importance of serving each other in the name of Jesus Christ; they show themselves to be willing to sacrifice themselves for each other to make their marriage holy. It is both a submission and a new birth, bonding with Christ in his eternal sacrifice for us.

I will share with you the story of a martyr from Iraq. In the heart of the ancient Nineveh city, Mosul, in 1972, a beautiful light named Ragheed Ganni was born. He completed a degree in civil engineering in 1993. Yet, the call of God could not be ignored. In 1996 he began a spiritual journey to Rome, surrounding himself with studies of philosophy and theology at the Irish College. Ordained in Rome in 2001, he returned to his birthplace, Mosul, filled with the Holy Spirit and with passion, generosity, and a deep love for the Church and his people. Even among the shadows of danger in Mosul, where the security situation was falling apart and forcing over 4,000 Christian families to consider escape, Father Ragheed's dedication never failed. He openly celebrated the Mass, constantly organised Christian education activities and youth gatherings, and ensured pastoral care for each person, in education, healthcare, catechism, and marriage.

2003 saw another dark era for Iraq. With the fall of the political regime the nation fell into chaos, becoming a playground for political and sectarian revenge.

Christians, already a minority, were persecuted by extremist Islamic groups, whilst organised crime spared no one. A mass exodus of Christians began; many found refuge in Kurdistan, hoping for a chance of safety, whilst a large number left Iraq altogether.

The historic city of Mosul in particular bore much hatred and anger, becoming a total landscape of fear. Threats followed people at every corner; kidnappings, killings based on one's faith, and cruel demands to seize homes from Christians became a harrowing kind of 'new normal'. Continuous bombings created a shadow so dark that the city felt like a prison, with no escape from threats and violence. Capturing this grim reality, Father Ragheed, in a heartfelt message to his mentor in Rome, Professor Robert Christian OP, shared something of the horror the day before he met his own tragic fate:

> The situation here is worse than hell, and my church has been attacked a few more times since we last met. Last week, two guards were wounded after an attack. We shall meet in the near future and have a chat about all these events.

In December 2004, the sacred grounds of Mosul's cathedral were attacked with explosions. By some divine miracle, Father Ragheed survived. But he knew that he was on a journey of martyrdom as he was not going to let the Church be broken. Speaking of this terrifying experience to a friend, he said,

Emerging alive, by the grace of God, I saw an untouched wall in the cathedral's reception. On it remained two unyielding symbols: the holy cross and the revered image of Pope John Paul II. It was a revelation – these evildoers can shatter stones, but they can never break the Church, the eternal sanctuary of God.

As a leader of the persecuted Church in Mosul, Father Ragheed knew he was facing death at any moment, and that the persecution would not spare his young life, especially as he continued to celebrate the Mass. He wrote his last prayer on 12 October 2006:

Lord, I don't think they will see my prayer as a pessimistic one, for everyone knew me as an optimist.

Perhaps, momentarily, they wondered about my optimism, for they saw me in the harshest of situations, smiling, encouraging, and strong.

But when they recall the times of hardship I lived, and the difficulties I went through, those that showed my weakness and your strength, my fragility, and your might, they'll know that I, my Hope, always spoke of you.

Because I truly knew you, and you were the reason for my optimism, even when I realized that my death was near.

But let me be with you now, as I have a hope to place before you.

You know better than me the times in which we

live, and I know how weak humans are. I want you to be my strength, and I won't let anyone disrespect the priesthood I bear.

Help me not to weaken and surrender myself out of fear for my life.

For I wish to die for you, to live with you and in you.

I am now ready to meet you.

Help me not to weaken during the trial.

For I've told you that I know humans, but I've also said that I know you. My Strength... My Might... My Hope.

He wrote as if to someone he knew and loved. In that process of sheer honesty it was cathartic: a purging, a purifying, a cleansing. Reassurances and strength came through the graces that were given to him to continue his mission, which would ultimately lead to martyrdom.

Father Ragheed drew his strength from the Eucharist as he wrote,

Due to the continuous attacks, whether they affected me directly or indirectly, I felt my own weakness and incapable of continuing with my duty. This peaked when I received a warning of a terrorist attack on my church, one hour before the Christmas Eve Mass, at a time when the church was packed. I felt very weak then. And when I lifted the host during the communion rite, equivalent to *This is the Lamb of God who takes away the sins of the world*, I really felt the Lord telling me that just as I carry him in my hands, so he carries us. The strength that overwhelmed me was the strength of his immense, boundless love, this love that enveloped me and all those who called upon him and sought his help.

Some eight months later, on 3 June 2007, Father Ragheed and three deacons were leaving the church after Mass; four gunmen approached them and told him that they had ordered him to close his church. He responded, 'How can I close the house of God?' They shot Father Ragheed and the deacons, filling their car with explosives so that no one could reach them.

The world lost that beautiful light that had come into the world thirty-five years earlier. I lost a dear friend and a brother in Christ. Sixteen years have passed. We have had the Islamic State, but the blood of the martyrs and our survivors are truly the seeds of the Church. Life is ever challenging for persecuted Christians. There are major difficulties with unemployment and healthcare, and costs of food and clothing can be difficult. Yet the churches are full as we work like Father Ragheed with hearts for our flock. We know each of our sheep as the true shepherd should.

Father Ragheed's story is just one story of martyrdom in a land where since 2003 over 1,200 Christians from all denominations have been brutally murdered: Bishop Faraj Rahho, Father Paulus Iskander, Father

Thaaer Wasim, Father Nabil, Pastor Mundhir al-Saqqa, Father Yousif Aboudi, Tha'ir Sa'ad Abdulahad Abdul, and Father Wasim Sabih Yousif al-Qas are the names of just a few.

To witness to Christ is a treasure beyond all value which we hold deep in our souls. We should be prepared to give our bodies to the head of the Church; this was the example that motivated all of us to stay and fight the good fight, as Christ must be witnessed to in Iraq.[2] And the priest must be there to be the shepherd. In Erbil, Kurdistan, we have built many structures in our Christian quarter to keep Christianity in Iraq, not least through the support of Christian agencies: a seminary, six churches, four schools, the Catholic University, a hospital. We still need help, but we always have hope and faith in the Holy Spirit.

Father Ragheed and each of the ten modern martyrs are examples of the Lord's blessings. They tasted and saw the goodness of the Lord, and purified themselves just as he is pure, and washed their robes and made them white in the blood of the Lamb (Revelation 7:14). That is why we celebrate and honour their love for Christ without tears, since God himself wiped away every tear from our eyes (Revelation 7:17). Let us ask for their prayers for peace in the world today.

Notes

Introduction

1 'World Watch List 2024: Trends', Open Doors, www.opendoorsuk.org/persecution/persecution-trends/, accessed 29 Apr 2024.

2 Address by Pope Francis at the Vatican Apostolic Palace, 11 May 2023, press.vatican.va/content/salastampa/en/bollettino/ pubblico/2023/05/11/230511a.html, accessed 10 Jan 2024.

3 WA Muniments, Acts of Chapter, 20 Jul 1993, item 3.2.

4 All of the correspondence, together with extensive notes on the entire project, can be found in WA Muniments, G/01/23–32.

5 Donald Buttress, 'Notes on Architectural Matters: The Martyrs', WA Muniments, SBU/04/01/003.

6 Published by Cassell in 1998.

7 'The King and Faith', The Royal Household, www.royal.uk/ the-king-and-faith, accessed 29 Apr 2024.

Maximilian Kolbe

1 Based on a sermon preached at Westminster Abbey on 22 Oct 2023. The readings for evensong were Psalm 85; Proverbs 4:1–18; John 15:1–17.

2 Part of the text used by Pope St John Paul II in his homily at Kolbe's canonisation.

3 Recounted in Regis J. Armstrong and Ingrid J. Peterson, *The Franciscan Tradition: Spirituality in History* (Collegeville, MN, 2010), 50.

4   Claude R. Foster, *Mary's Knight: The Mission and Martyrdom of Saint Maksymilian Maria Kolbe* (West Chester, PA, 2002).

5   Quoted in Emmanuel Abur, *Tales of Agonies: A Psycho-Spiritual Prism* (New York, 2023), 86.

6   Antonio Tarallo, 'St. Maximilian Kolbe's life as a child prepared him for a path to holiness', Catholic News Agency (14 Aug 2023), accessed online 30 Oct 2023.

7   Homily of Pope John Paul II, St Peters Square, 10 Oct 1982, www.vatican.va/content/john-paul-ii/it/homilies/1982/documents/hf_jp-ii_hom_19821010_canonizzazione-kolbe.html, accessed 30 Oct 2023.

8   Ibid.

9   Maximilian M. Kolbe, *Positio super virtutibus: Responsio ad Animadversiones,* Vol. I (Rome, 1966), 139.

10 Quoted in translation in Zdzisław Józef Kijas, 'The process of Beatification and Canonisation of Maximilian Maria Kolbe', *Studia Elbląskie*, XXI (2020).

11 Homily of Pope John Paul II, St Peters Square, 10 Oct 1982.

Manche Masemola

1   Based on a sermon preached at Westminster Abbey on 29 Oct 2023. The readings for evensong were Psalm 142; Ecclesiastes 11–12; 2 Timothy 2:1–7.

2   For background and for the few details we know, see: Mandy Goedhals, 'Imperialism, mission and conversion: Manche Masemola of Sekhukhuneland' in Andrew Chandler (ed.), *The Terrible Alternative: Christian Martyrdom in the Twentieth Century* (London, 1998), 28–45.

3   Ibid., 37.

4   Manche Masemola Pilgrimage 2020, Anglican Church of Southern Africa, anglicanchurchsa.org/wp-content/uploads/2020/07/Manche_Masemola_pilgrimage_2020.pdf, accessed 20 Oct 2023.

5 Ailred of Rievaulx, quoted in Richard Mortimer, *Edward the Confessor: The Man and the Legend* (Woodbridge, 2009), 174.

Janani Luwum

1 Based on a sermon preached at Westminster Abbey on 19 Nov 2023. The readings for evensong were Psalm 119:145–160; 2 Chronicles 24:17–21; Revelation 1:4–18.
2 Michela Wrong, 'Why were 80,000 Asians suddenly expelled from Uganda in 1972?', *The Spectator* (26 Aug 2023).
3 'How many people did Amin really kill?', *Monitor Uganda* (27 Sep 2012), www.monitor.co.ug/uganda/special-reports/uganda-50/how-many-people-did-amin-really-kill--1526590, accessed 30 Apr 2024.
4 John Sentamu, 'Tribalism, religion and despotism in Uganda: Archbishop Janini Luwum' in Chandler (ed.), *The Terrible Alternative*, 156.
5 Ibid., 147.
6 Quoted in ibid., 148.
7 Ibid., 145.
8 Ibid., 146.
9 'Martyrdom is the ultimate witness to Christ's truth', archbishopofcanterbury.org (17 Feb 2016), www.archbishopofcanterbury.org/martyrdom-ultimate-witness-christs-truth, accessed 17 Nov 2023.

Elizabeth of Russia

1 Based on a sermon preached at Westminster Abbey on 1 Oct 2023. The readings for evensong were Psalm 8; Ezekiel 37:15–28; Luke 23:32–43.
2 'Mountbatten Papers: Recollections of Victoria, Marchioness of Milford Haven', Broadlands Archives, University of Southampton Special Collections, MS62/MB/21, 125, accessed 20 Sep 2023.

3   Maurice Paléologue, *The Memoirs of Maurice Paléologue at the Russian Court of Nicholas II*, Vol. I (Winter Palace Publishing [n.p.], 2018), 185–6.

4   Desmond Tutu, *No Future Without Forgiveness* (New York, 1999), 22.

5   One of those who records this saying is Elizabeth's former mistress of the robes, Countess Alexandra Olsoufieff, in *Palace Personalities: HIH Grand Duchess Elisabeth Feodorovna* (London, 1923).

6   See Kara Smith's dissertation, 'A legacy of care: Hesse and the Alice Frauenverein, 1867–1918' [thesis], ir.ua.edu/handle/123456789/778, accessed 20 Sep 2023.

7   'Mountbatten Papers', Broadlands Archives, 143.

Martin Luther King Jr

1   Based on a sermon preached at Westminster Abbey on 10 Oct 2023. The readings for evensong were Psalms 53 and 54; 1 Kings 22:1–28; Romans 15:4–13.

2   Honorary degree ceremony for Martin Luther King Jr, Newcastle University (13 Nov 1967), youtu.be/TwXfITDyIuY, accessed 9 Apr 2024.

3   Martin Luther King, 'Letter from Birmingham Jail' [open letter], 18 April 1963.

4   'From Lament to Action', Archbishops' Antiracism Taskforce (22 Apr 2021), www.churchofengland.org/sites/default/files/2021-04/FromLamentToAction-report.pdf, accessed 27 Feb 2024.

5   Words by King used within the Macpherson report (2019) into the murder of Stephen Lawrence as a definition of 'institutional racism' and subsequently adopted by the Archbishops' Anti-Racism Taskforce report, 'From Lament to Action'.

6   King, 'Letter from Birmingham Jail'.

Óscar Romero

1 Based on a sermon preached at Westminster Abbey on 10 Sep 2023. The readings for evensong were Psalm 54; Ezekiel 12:21–13:16; Acts 19:1–20.

2 Philip Berryman, 'The Oppression of the People: Archbishop Oscar Romero of El Salvador' in Chandler (ed.), *The Terrible Alternative*, 174.

3 Ibid., 174.

4 Seàn-Patrick Lovett, 'Remembering St Oscar Romero: 40 years after his assassination', Vatican News (24 Mar 2020), accessed online 8 September 2023.

5 Óscar Romero, *The Scandal of Redemption: When God Liberates the Poor, Saves Sinners, and Heals Nations*, ed. by Carolyn Kurtz (Robertsbridge, 2018), 20.

6 Lovett, 'Remembering St Oscar Romero'.

7 Richard Harries, *Faith in Politics* (London, 2010).

8 Romero, *The Scandal of Redemption*, 11.

9 Ibid., 122.

10 Roberto Morozzo Della Rocca, *Oscar Romero: Prophet of Hope* (London, 2015), 223–4.

11 Ibid., 224.

12 Michael Lapsley, 'Foreword' in Romero, *The Scandal of Redemption*, x.

13 Quoted in ibid., xi.

Dietrich Bonhoeffer

1 Based on a sermon preached at Westminster Abbey on 17 Sep 2023. The readings for evensong were Psalm 89:1–16; Ezekiel 20:1–8, 33–44; Acts 20:17–38.

2 Eric Metaxas, *Bonhoeffer: Pastor, Martyr, Prophet, Spy* (London, 2010), 4.

3 Dietrich Bonhoeffer, *Letters and Papers from Prison*, ed. by Bethge Eberhard (London, 2017), 4.

4   Ibid., 28.

5   Ibid., 18.

6   Sam Wells, 'Foreword' in ibid, xiii.

7   Ibid., 52.

8   Ibid., 149.

9   Ibid., 149.

10   'Bishop of Truro's Independent Review for the Foreign Secretary of FSO Support for Persecuted Christians: Final Report and Recommendations', christianpersecutionreview. org.uk, accessed online 27 Feb 2024.

Esther John

1   Based on a sermon preached at Westminster Abbey on 26 Nov 2023. The readings for evensong were Psalm 93; 1 Maccabees 2:15–29; Matthew 28:16–20.

2   'UK Martyrs of the modern era', BBC News (9 Jul 1998), news.bbc.co.uk/1/hi/uk/129587.stm, accessed 20 Nov 2023.

3   Patrick Sookhdeo, 'Mission and conversion in Pakistan: Esther John (Qamar Zia)' in Chandler (ed.), *The Terrible Alternative*, 110.

4   Ibid., 110

5   Anglican Communion Network for Inter Faith Concerns (NIFCON), *Generous Love: the truth of the Gospel and the call to dialogue* (London, 2008), 12.

6   Sookhdeo, 'Mission and conversion in Pakistan', 113.

7   Ibid., 114.

8   'Update: Pakistani churches meet outside after devastating attacks', Open Doors, www.opendoorsuk.org/news/latest-news/pakistan-mob/, accessed 20 Nov 2023.

9   'Tertullian (145–220): Apology', translated by S. Thelwall, logoslibrary.org, Chapter 50, accessed 29 Apr 2024.

Lucian Tapiedi

1 Based on a sermon preached at Westminster Abbey on 17 Dec 2023. The readings for evensong were Psalm 111; Malachi 3:1–4, 4; Acts 7:51–60.

2 Robert Leckie, *Helmet for My Pillow: From Parris Island to the Pacific* (Toronto, 1958), 52.

3 David Wetherell (ed.), *The New Guinea Diaries of Philip Strong, 1936–1945* (London, 1981), 46.

Wang Zhiming

1 Based on a sermon preached at Westminster Abbey on 24 Sep 2023. The readings for evensong were Psalm 119:1–16; Ezekiel 33:23, 30–34; Acts 26:1, 9–25.

2 Philip L. Wickeri, 'The abolition of religion in Yunan: Wang Zhiming' in Chandler (ed.) *The Terrible Alternative*, 128–143, 134.

3 Ibid., 137.

4 Ibid., 138.

5 Liao Yiwu, *God is Red: The Secret Story of How Christianity Survived and Flourished in Communist China* (London, 2012), 108; Wickeri, 'The Abolution of Religion', 138.

God Will Wipe Away Every Tear

1 Homily preached on All Saints' Day, 1 Nov 2023. The readings at the sung Eucharist were Revelation 7:9–17; 1 John 3:1–3; Matthew 5:1–12.

2 St Augustine writes of the *totus Christus*, the 'whole Christ', head and body together.

HAUS CURIOSITIES

Inspired by the topical pamphlets of the interwar years, as well as by Einstein's advice to 'never lose a holy curiosity', the series presents short works of opinion and analysis by notable figures. Under the guidance of the series editor, Peter Hennessy, Haus Curiosities have been published since 2014.

Welcoming contributions from a diverse pool of authors, the series aims to reinstate the concise and incisive booklet as a powerful strand of politico-literary life, amplifying the voices of those who have something urgent to say about a topical theme.

A Love Affair with Europe: The Case for a European Future
Giles Radice

Fiction, Fact and Future: The Essence of EU Democracy
James Elles

We Are the People: The Rise of the AfD in Germany
Penny Bochum

Citizens of Everywhere: Searching for Identity in the Age of Brexit
Peter Gumbel

The London Problem: What Britain Gets Wrong About its Capital City
Jack Brown

Unwritten Rule: How to Fix the British Constitution
Stephen Green, Thomas Legg, and Martin Donnelly

HAUS CURIOSITIES
PUBLISHED WITH THE WESTMINSTER ABBEY INSTITUTE

Trust in Public Life
Anna Rowlands, Claire Gilbert, Josie Rourke, Anthony Ball, and James Hawkey

Justice in Public Life
Anna Rowlands, Claire Gilbert, Josie Rourke, Anthony Ball, and James Hawkey

The Power of Politicians
Tessa Jowell and Frances D'Souza

The Power of Civil Servants
David Normington and Peter Hennessy

The Power of Judges
David Neuberger and Peter Riddell

The Power of Journalists
Nick Robinson, Gary Gibbon, Barbara Speed, and
Charlie Beckett

The Responsibilities of Democracy
John Major and Nick Clegg

Integrity in Public Life
Vernon White, Claire Foster-Gilbert, and Jane Sinclair

Truth in Public Life
Vernon White, Stephen Lamport, and Claire Foster-Gilbert

Secret Service
Jonathan Evans

Art, Imagination and Public Service
David Blunkett, Micheal O'Siadhail, Brenda Hale,
Hughie O'Donoghue, Clare Moriarty, and James O'Donnell